Patrick Skinner's Cyprus Kitchen

Patrick Skinner and his wife Mary settled in Cyprus in 1991, "to live a quieter rural life", he to write about wine, she to develop the house and garden of their hillside retreat. This followed some years of running an international marketing and PR firm, which entailed much writing: articles, speeches, reports, books, TV documentaries and people profiles. The pen, typewriter and word processor have assisted multi-national corporations, hotels, airlines, tourism organisations, food manufacturers, wine producers and wine marketeers from all over the world.

He now writes every week on food and drink in "The Cyprus Mail", has a widely syndicated weekly column about Mediterranean food and contributes to many magazines in Cyprus and elsewhere. When not writing he helps Mary run the "Friends of the Cyprus Donkey" sanctuary, which, since it was founded in 1994 has taken in more than 130 unwanted animals. Every copy of this book sold will provide a donation for the sanctuary.

Alyana Cazalet was born in Russia and studied art in Moscow and London. She published two books in Russia, "School" (1989) and "Quiet Feasts" (1991). After moving to London she worked as a freelance artist and illustrator, including assignments for a BBC children's magazine. Her work has been exhibited in Britain, France and Spain. She moved to Cyrus in 1995, where she has continued her work, undertaking various projects, participating in several exhibitions and has had her own one woman show in 1998. She has been inspired by the colour and taste of Cyprus food. She admits not to have tried any of Patrick's recipes as yet – which will mark yet another turning point in her varied and interesting life.

Patrick Skinner's Cyprus Kitchen

Illustrated by Alyana Cazalet

Home cooking from the Mediterranean and one or two other places
A Cyprus **Mail** Book

A *Cyprus* **Mail** Publication

First published in Cyprus in 1998 by
Cyprus Mail Co Ltd.
24 Vassiliou Voulgaroctonou
P.O. Box 1144, Nicosia, Cyprus

Text Copyright © 1998 Patrick Skinner
Drawings (except where otherwise indicated) Copyright © 1998 Alyana Cazalet
Text body and headlines computer-set in Goudy Old Style

ISBN 9963 - 8377 - 0 - 0

Menu

Stocks & Sauces 23

Soups, Starters & Mezeses 43

Pasta 63

Fish 77

Beef 95

Pork 111

Menu 2

Lamb	121
Chicken, Turkey & Rabbit	129
Salads	153
Rice	165
Vegetables	177
Puddings	193

Before we start...

How it all came about

The first meal I can remember *properly* was when I was four. My brother, then 13, was going camping a mile or so away from our house, carrying his tent, supper, "Billy" can and bedding on his bicycle. As a treat, I was allowed to walk alongside, with MY supper and spend an hour or two before my father came to collect me and take me home to bed. In grease-proof paper were some slices of fresh ham, cut from gammon on the bone, a tomato, some cucumber, some bread and butter, and, miracle of miracles, a small bottle of Heinz tomato ketchup. I can remember -- and still enjoy -- the flavours of good ham and tomato ketchup to this day. I also remember crying loudly when my father came to collect me.

I was a sickly child and the Belgian doctor who advised our family said that I should have "nourishing" food: little milk, but plenty of vegetables and meat. I rapidly got to know the ingredients of what my mother used to cook. Often this was vegetable soup, which she pressed, by hand, through a sieve. I still make this sort of soup, but today have the benefit of a food processor to turn it into whatever thickness of purée I want. I got to asking her to vary the taste a little from day to day, and became aware of Marmite as flavouring in soups. As I got into my teens I became more robust but my interest in food remained. It was war-time and nobody was very interested in children: fathers and brothers were at the front or flying, and many of them lost their lives. There were no stress counsellors, youth leaders or anybody else to bring us up, so we wandered the streets, often receiving chewing gum, candy, biscuits, tins of Spam, fruit juice and so on from passing American army trucks full of soldiers. They added to the variety of drab war-time rations.

Sometimes when I came home from school in the afternoon my mother would be out and I would be alone, my father and sister being away and my brother having been killed in Egypt in 1941. She would leave me various things on the kitchen table: salad, potatoes, Spam or American sausage meat (she had quite a few American admirers stationed not far away from where we lived). I soon learnt that the fat from around the sausages, an excellent quality of lard, could be boiled up, cleared of bits of sausage and used to fry potatoes (clarified it could even be used in cakes!); and that egg (even dried egg), a little water and milk would make a sort of batter that would coat slices of Spam and could be fried. I didn't invent the Spam Fritter, but I was right in there at the start of something that went on for years. I used to sit having my tea dreaming of cooking, of running a restaurant, although what recipes I could think of at the time escape me now. Spam would probably have figured quite large.

There were treats... sometimes I would get to go to London, even travelling alone through it in the Doodlebug era, aged 13, on the way from Scotland and a visit to my father, to Torquay and Mama, and having my supper at Lyons Brasserie in Coventry Street (Reindeer steak and chips!) There were family outings sometimes and the high-spot for me was always a restaurant. And there were chippies. I would often go, by myself, or with a few shillings from one of Mama's boy friends to get enough for them. You'd stand in line for half an hour or so to be rewarded by a chunk of fresh fish in batter and chips. I sat on my bike and golloped mine before taking the rest home. There were other things that helped stetched the basic rations, like tea-shops, where scones and home-made cakes could be had. The times were exciting and taught self-reliance and enterprise.

Whatever my mother's proclivities were, she provided well. Ever flirtatious, butchers were charmed and gave her liver, kidney and other offal which wasn't on ration. Heinz Baked Beans and Spaghetti were on coupons called "Points" and it was surprising how often an extra tin was slipped into her shopping bag. The war came to an end and my parents' enforced separation ended, too.

With the return of family life, I watched my mother get the Sunday roast. Although her cooking was English and not wide-ranging, what she did she did very well, and I learnt to coincide the ingredients of a Sunday meal so that each part came to the table at its best: get the meat in for an hour and a half or so. At one hour to serving add the potatoes. At 45 minutes (having made it beforehand), beat the Yorkshire pudding mixture again and put it in around the meat. Fifteen minutes, boil the vegetables and make the gravy. To cook you need a timer or a built-in clock, and fortunately, as far as food is concerned, I have the latter, especially when it comes to the time of eating! Wherever I am in the world I want lunch at 1 and dinner between 7.30 and 8.00 pm (even if I have been flying all night).

My mother used to go away a lot, to see my sister, a repertory actress, and one day, as she left, she wrote down the recipe for Yorkshire pudding. I cooked it under the beef that Sunday, to my father's delectation and after that there was no stopping me. It was batter with everything: apples, sausages, mixed vegetables, lamb chops... My father couldn't cook and was no gastronome, but he liked his meat and tatties, so we got on well.

Through my first marriage and subsequent widespread business travel I learnt about Middle Eastern food, having had preliminary skirmishes with curry of sorts during National Service in the RAF and an occasional visit to Veeraswamy's Indian restaurant in Regent Street, London. I loved the rice, I loved the cracked wheat, I loved the yogurt, I loved the sauces, the fresh vegetables and delicious recipes with minced meat, and I loved the fresh fish of the Mediterranean.

I began to cook a lot at home and, when I married for the second time, to a *very* good cook of the French style, working together in business meant sharing duties and I happily took on the tasks of shopping and cooking. So I learnt to cook quickly, when arriving home at half past seven at night, for children and ourselves. More travel in relation to our work brought new culinary experiences.

In my younger days I was very heavy on certain ingredients, especially spices and garlic, and our children were often chided at school following an evening when they had eaten spaghetti bolognese liberally laced with the good clove or three.

I started keeping recipes culled from magazines and newspapers, and then I started writing down my own variations. An impatient person, I was soon making up my own, which re-appeared if those round the table approved.

On settling in Cyprus in 1991, to live more quietly and to write about wine, I started writing the occasional article for British magazines and, after a while, I noticed a free monthly newspaper called The Cyprus Sun and that its first issue contained no article about the wines of Cyprus, which I had been assiduously tasting and making notes about for some months. I telephoned the editor, the dear and sadly late Tony Purdy. I enquired why they hadn't got a wine column. "I haven't got a wine writer," he replied. My response was short and to the point. "You have now." The following month my first survey of Cyprus wines came out. It was not too many months before the continental lady who wrote the food column departed and Tony asked me if I would take on food as well. I accepted with alacrity, but then came a snag: I knew so many dishes inside out; I made them regularly, but the quantities of ingredients? The cooking times? I knew none of these. So I had to go back to my own school and cook my own recipes, noting down the quantities, the method, the timing and so on.

For 18 lovely months I enjoyed writing for The Cyprus Sun and, because it had a large circulation, I made many friends. Then, of course, because it didn't have enough advertising, it folded. But then Sir Galahad, in the form of Kyriacos Jacovides, the Managing Director of the Cyprus Mail, came galloping over the horizon. Would I do a half page of food and wine notes in the Cyprus Mail on Sunday? Would I not?

A few more months of this and the restaurant critic retired, so, with some help from fellow reviewers, I took this on as well and, in a re-organisation, was handed two pages.

All this meant that the food file on the computer was getting fatter and fatter and, with the aid of super-secretary Sue Kyriacou, these were put in order. "You ought to produce a cook book," I had been told many times. So, with the co-operation of the Cyprus Mail, who have published this little tome, I have.

A Word about Cooking

The axiom, "If you love food you will enjoy cooking," does not hold true. I know gourmets who can't boil an egg. And I also know some dreadful cooks who love food.

A lot of people have to follow recipes, and there is nothing wrong in this, whilst others are improvisational, or read a recipe and then adapt it for themselves. I am largely in the latter category, and as I have always been in a hurry I have tried to compile recipes that are relatively simple to prepare and to cook and serve.

It may be that to you cooking is a bore, or a chore. So in my recipes I have tried to present a selection of simple, straightforward dishes with a dash of the Mediterranean, a pinch of Oriental spice and a hint or two of other areas of this globe of ours interspersed, that you will enjoy eating. I want to try and convey my enjoyment in preparing these recipes, too.

Then, you may have hundreds of cookbooks and this one will be an addition to browse through from time to time. Or you may have none at all, and for this reason I have included notes about weights and measures, utensils and basic methods, as well as recipes for the simplest and most basic of stocks and sauces.

Not my kitchen - a 16th century engraving of a chef in his kitchen. Untidy, perhaps, but everything is to hand.

I have loved every minute of a lifetime of enjoying food, and especially of cooking it, writing about it, and serving it to family and friends. I hope that just a touch of this enjoyment may be yours in reading this book and hopefully using it with success. And remember...

If you think it's going to take an hour, allow an hour and a half.
Cook within your capabilities -- better something simple that's good than an elaborate disaster.
When trying out a new dish, try it out on your family before doing it for a dinner party and worrying about your guests' reactions.

Temperatures, Weights and Measures

Throughout the book I have used metric measurements, with the occasional exception of the phrase "cup" or "coffee cup", which I have not converted because of the ease with which one can use these implements. Most people today have electronic or very good counter-sprung scales and many have both grams and pounds and ounces. However, where conversion is necessary, I have tried to give complete tables, which are on the following pages. The section is concluded with the abbreviations used throughout.

Weight
The metric unit is the kilogram (kg), which equals 1000 grams (g) or approximately 2 lb 4 oz.

Metric	UK/US	Metric	UK/US
25 g	1 oz	400 g	14 oz
50 g	2 oz	425 g	15 oz
75 g	3 oz	450 g	16 oz (1 lb)
100-125 g	4 oz	500 g (½ kg)	17½ oz
150 g	5 oz	1 kg	2.2 lb
175 g	6 oz	1.5 kg	3.3 lb
200 g	7 oz	2 kg	4.4 lb
225 g	8 oz	2.5 kg	5.5 lb
250 g	9 oz	3 kg	6.6 lb
275 g	10 oz	3.5 kg	7.7 lb
300 g	11 oz	4 kg	8.8 lb
325-350 g	12 oz	4.5 kg	9.9 lb
		5 kg	11 lb

Oven Temperatures
The table below is an approximate guide.

Faranheit	Centigrade/Celcius	Gas Number	Oven Heat
225	110	¼	very cool
250	130	½	very cool
275	140	1	cool
300	150	2	slow
325	170	3	moderately slow
350	180	4	moderate
375	190	5	moderately hot
400	200	6	hot
425	220	7	very hot

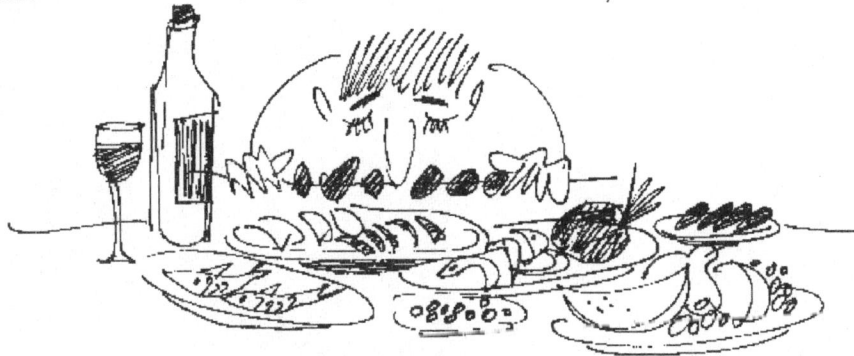

Liquids

Metric	UK	US
30 ml	1 fl oz	2 tbsp
60 ml	2 fl oz	½ cup
80 ml	3 fl oz	⅓ cup
100 ml	3½ fl oz	coffee cup
125 ml	4 fl oz	½ cup
160 ml	5 fl oz	⅔ cup
180 ml	6 fl oz	¾ cup
250 ml	8 fl oz	1 cup
375 ml	12 fl oz	1½ cups
500 ml	16 fl oz	2 cups
1 litre	32 fl oz	4 cups/1 qt

Length

Cake, bread and biscuit tins, kitchen foil and similar items are sold in metres (m), equalling 100 centimetres (cm) or 1000 millimetres (mm). The metre equals 1 yd 3 in.

Metric	UK/US		Metric	UK/US
3 mm	⅛ in		4.5 cm	1¾ in
5mm	¼ in		5 cm	2 in
10 mm (1 cm)	½ in		10 cm	4 in
2 cm	¾ in		20.5 cm	8 in
2.5 cm	1 in		30.5 cm	12 in (1 ft)
3 cm	1¼ in		91.5 cm	36 in (1 yd)
4 cm	1½ in		100 cm (1 m)	39 in

Useful Equivalents

Plain (All-Purpose) Flour/Dried Bread Crumbs/Chopped Nuts

Metric	UK	US
30 g	1 oz	¼ cup
45 g	1½ oz	⅓ cup
60 g	2 oz	½ cup
90 g	3 oz	¾ cup
125 g	4 oz	1 cup
185 g	6 oz	1½ cup
250 g	8 oz	2 cups

Jam/Honey

Metric	UK	US
60 g	2 oz	2 tbsp
90 g	3 oz	¼ cup
155 g	5 oz	½ cup
250 g	8 oz	¾ cup
345 g	11 oz	1 cup

White Sugar

Metric	UK	US
60 g	2 oz	¼ cup
90 g	3 oz	⅓cup
125 g	4 oz	½ cup
185 g	6 oz	¾ cup
250 g	8 oz	1 cup
375 g	12 oz	1½ cups
500 g	1 lb	2 cups

Whole-Wheat (Wholemeal) Flour

Metric	UK	US
30 g	1 oz	3 tbsp
60 g	2 oz	½ cup
90 g	3 oz	⅔ cup
125 g	4 oz	1 cup
155 g	5 oz	1¼ cups
210 g	7 oz	1⅔ cups
250 g	8 oz	1¾ cups

Long-Grain Rice/Cornmeal

Metric	UK	US
60 g	2 oz	⅓ cup
75 g	2½ oz	½ cup
125 g	4 oz	¾ cup
155 g	5 oz	1 cup
250 g	8 oz	1½ cups

Dried Beans

Metric	UK	US
45 g	1½ oz	¼ cup
60 g	2 oz	⅓ cup
90 g	3 oz	½ cup
155 g	5 oz	¾ cup
185 g	6 oz	1 cup
250 g	8 oz	1¼ cups
375 g	12 oz	1½ cups

Grated Dry Cheese

Metric	UK	US
30 g	1 oz	¼ cup
60 g	2 oz	½ cup
90 g	3 oz	¾ cup
125 g	4 oz	1 cup
155 g	5 oz	1⅓ cups
220 g	7 oz	2 cups

Solid Measurements

UK	US
8 oz butter or fat	1 cup (solidly packed)
2 oz butter or fat	¼ cup (4 tablespoons)
8 oz caster sugar	1 cup plus 3 tablespoons
2 oz caster sugar	4 tablespoons
1 lb plain flour, sieved	4½ cups cake flour, sieved
4 oz plain flour, sieved	1 cup plus 4 tablespoons
1 oz plain flour, sieved	4 tablespoons

Abbreviations used in this book

cofsp	=	coffee spoon(s)
tsp	=	teaspoon(s)
des-sp	=	dessert spoon(s)
tbsp	=	tablespoon(s)
ml	=	millilitre(s)
cl	=	centilitre(s)
l	=	litres(s)
g	=	gramme(s)
k	=	kilogram(s)

My Kitchen

Many of us have the chance to re-equip a kitchen, but fewer the opportunity to build and design one from scratch. When we moved to Cyprus in 1991 this was our good fortune. I had previously cooked in kitchens ranging from very large, where there was quite a walk from one side to the other, to one that was little more than a galley in a 15th century house in Kent. In our Cyprus venture there was only one constraint: the room was four metres wide and eventually the kitchen came out almost square. It followed what I think are the golden rules.

Have a central working surface, plus plenty of other surfaces which can be used to work on. One of these should be very close, if not adjacent, to the hob.

Cooking pots and pans should be easily accessible, and I think they are best hanging overhead.

Ingredients should be kept fairly close together, so that you don't have to walk from one side of the kitchen to the other to get the flour, the oil, the currants and so on.

Have some good wooden working surfaces – I have had several "butcher's block" tops made for the central working table, and a side dresser. I do not advocate formica or similar laminates, which are very easy to cut. Where I do not have wood I have granite, which is a wonderful surface, but plays havoc with knives if you chop on it.

Have a floor that will resist dropped wine, tomato juice, Worcester sauce, oil, butter and other things that you will be throwing about when you are cooking. We have antique-finish terracotta tiles, which we brought from Spain and which are very kind-hearted and accommodating, especially as I am a slightly messy cook.

It is said you shouldn't have a refrigerator next to the cooker, but insulation is good in modern ovens and often there is very little alternative. I have to say that I have never had any problems, and having the 'fridge so close to the preparation surfaces is very handy.

Above all, be *comfortable* in your kitchen and remember you are undoubtedly going to spend more time in it than in your car -- and how much do you spend on, and how often do you change, *that?* Don't deny yourself the chance to equip it in the way that is going to please you. Eating and the preparation of what goes into it are, or should be, several of life's most satisfying activities.

Equipment

You can have electric woks, bread-makers, rice-cookers and lots of bolt-ons to give you ease of doing certain things, but I think the following are totally indispensable: *a medium to large sized food processor, a small food processor, and several electric coffee grinders.*

The large processor does the major mixing, cutting and shredding jobs; the small one makes mayonnaise, bread crumbs and modest quantities of dry or semi-dry mixes; whilst the smallest grinders are used for dried and fresh herbs, nuts, seeds etc. You can have an electric beater if you like, though a good food processor will make all the sponge and cake mixes you need, and for whipping cream a big whisk and a slack wrist will do the job as quickly as an electric doobry.

Another very useful electric tool is a "Minute Grill", which can make toasted sandwiches, defrost pitta bread and other things and cook superb steaks, fillets of chicken etc in a few minutes.

For anyone starting a kitchen, I think it is essential to have some very good quality pans that are durable and heavy; and, although they weigh a ton, I don't think you can beat Le Creuset saucepans, casseroles, paté makers etc.

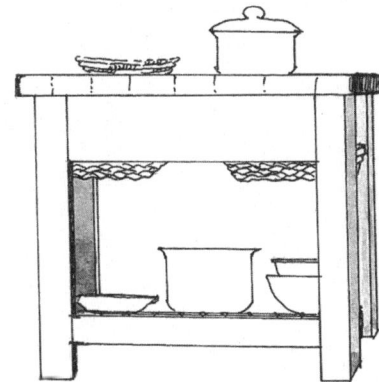

I think you also need a selection of fairly cheap non-stick pans, which one uses virtually every day and it is pointless paying £30-£40 for a frying pan only to have the non-stick surface come off in a few months. Better buy one for under £10, work it hard and throw it away when the non-stick surface gets scratched – as it surely will.

Scales. Mine are old-fashioned, just for fun, with both metric and pounds-and-ounces weights, because I still refer to recipe books, notably from America, where pounds-and-ounces prevail. If you can get an electronic balance with both metric and pounds-and-ounces, it will be useful. Otherwise use conversion tables. (See pages 8 - 13)

Baking dishes. I have never had ones that I think are well designed and made. Generally "non-stick" surfaces are not and cleaning is very difficult. So I think it is best to aim for good quality here and to search diligently for brands that seem to offer what you want. Then, only buy one item, to see if it is what you want!

Plus ça change - a kitchen in Pompeii two thousand years ago.

The Recipes and the Ingredients

You will note a distinctly Mediterranean flavour in both recipes and ingredients. Whilst I enjoy food from many climes, I think my first love is the cuisine of the Mediterranean region (which in itself is varied enough!). Hence, in my kitchen, there are always olive, ground nut and sunflower oils for cooking purposes and salad dressings. Then there are plenty of onions, garlic, tomatoes and herbs. The ingredients are those that are generally available, both in Cyprus and most other countries. I have tried not to mention exotic stuff that you can only find in a little shop in Soho or, So-Ho. Written in Cyprus, the book contains no mention of canned tomatoes in the recipes – the fresh ones here are perfect for cooking. But in other places, if you are using these recipes, unless you have plenty of ripe tomatoes, substitute the canned ones in all recipes. As for herbs, they are not widely used in Cyprus, except the bay leaf in dishes like stifado, but I am very fond of them and herbs grow excellently here. I prefer to use fresh wherever possible, because the ones in

One of the nicest ways to grow herbs for culinary use is in window boxes. Several varieties can grow happily in just one.

jars and packets lose their flavour very quickly unless you are cooking for a lot of people regularly, or are heavy handed with them. Thus, outside my back door and around the garden there are: mint, chives (quite difficult in this country to keep going year after year), parsley, sage, rosemary, thyme, oregano and bay. They are very fragrant and only a small amount is needed to give an excellent flavour. It's easy to have a herb garden wherever you live, and I had a fine one in Kent before we moved to Cyprus, so I do advocate fresh herbs if you can manage them.

I am also a firm advocate of alcohol in cooking. All kinds add depth and flavour to a recipe: red and white wines, vermouths, brandy, beer, whisky; and in puddings, brandy again, and liqueurs. Of course, in Cyprus, we are very lucky in that all these things are very inexpensive and we can slosh them about with gay abandon. As for the recipes . . .

Tip: Buy fresh. Buy frequently, if you can. Look for the markets and the produce which has come in from smallholders. Go to supermarkets on days you know fresh produce is coming in.

I have tried to present a cross-section of dishes that will give variation through the year and also, hopefully, balanced meals, whether they are two or three courses or a buffet. I am nearly always in a hurry, so simplicity in cooking is essential and you will see that a lot of suggestions can be cooked in well under an hour, and many in half an hour. I have tried to make each recipe as simple as possible to follow and to present the ingredients and the method in as close to the cooking order as I can. Another point to remember is that things vary. Unless you are buying for a top class hotel or restaurant in considerable quantities and can specify the exact size and condition of your ingredients, everything changes, often from day to day – even water and milk. Cooks change from day to day, too. Results, therefore, vary from time to time, place to place, and person to person. The purpose of a recipe is to provide something that can be followed exactly if you wish, but which can also be adapted to your own needs. If you don't like a herb, a spice or another ingredient in a recipe, remember – it's not written in concrete! The aim of cooking is not only to nourish, it is to please; you, and the people around your table. So don't hesitate to change, adapt and improvise. Your cooking will be the better for it.

Stocks and Sauces

Stocks & Sauces

Aïoli... Page 27
Barbecue Sauce .... Page 31
Bechamel.. Page 40
Brown Stock... Page 25
Chicken and Meat Stock .... Page 25
Egg & Parsley Sauce .... Page 41
Fish Stock... Page 26
Herb Sauce .... Page 42
Marinade .... Page 31
Mayonnaise .... Page 27
Mushroom Sauce .... Page 32
Mustard Sauce.. Page 33
Quick Mustard Sauce .... Page 34
Onion Marmalade .... Page 30
Ragu alla Bolognese .... Page 36
Remoulade .... Page 34
Skordalia (Garlic Sauce) .... Page 29
Tartare Sauce .... Page 28
Tomato Chutney .... Page 38
Tomato Sauce .... Page 35
Vegetable Stock .... Page 26
White Sauce .... Page 39

Chicken & Meat Stock

During a visit to the UK I was astonished at how tasteless chicken was and was glad to get back to the Cyprus variety. I always have one in fridge or freezer and a good bird does for several days, as they say, providing the basis for a number of meals. I always start by boiling the fowl, with a few off-cuts of bacon or ham, a celery stick, an onion, a carrot and fresh thyme, which produces super stock. It can always be removed about fifteen minutes before it's fully tender, stuffed with a pre-cooked 'farce' and browned in a very hot oven if you like.

The stock enables you to produce a huge pan of delicious rice pilaff, which fills the blighters up, accompanied by a home-made tomato sauce and, say, pork chops.

Of the stock that remains, cooked bones can be added to make a mixed meat stock. Don't add pepper to a stock, put it in when you use it.

A Stock Pot

A family job, really! Left-overs, bones, vegetable remains (clean, of course!), a drop of wine, herbs from the allotment and lots more can keep a stock pot going semi-permanently, topped up and boiled up daily and kept in a cool place.

Brown Stock

Invaluable for good stews and casseroles, gravy, too. Ask the butcher for veal and beef bones -- a pork one or two won't go amiss -- and have him chop them into hand-size pieces. Bake in the oven until the meaty remnants are brown.

In a large pot, stir-fry for a few minutes, in a little oil, some onions, celery, carrots and other bits and bobs of veggies that are handy, with some chopped up bacon. Put in plenty of water and add the baked bones, some seasoning and either a bouquet garni or a few good pinches of fresh sage, thyme, bay, parsley and oregano. Cover and simmer for several hours. This stock may be put in small containers and frozen.

Vegetable Stock

Folk often look blank at the words "Vegetable Stock"— at least the carnivores among us do— but a good one can greatly enhance a number of dishes and is easier and less messy to make than any other. And you can play about with leaf and root veggies and herbs to get the right one for the occasion.

Basically, we are talking about equal weights, say 250 grams, each of onions, carrots and celery, plus other vegetables you have to hand—a leaf or two of cabbage, a small head of fennel, a chopped leek, a tomato if you want some colour, plus some parsley, a garlic clove, some coriander seeds, a bay leaf and a pinch or two of fresh herbs, such as thyme, rosemary and sage.

Add all these to a litre and a half of water, with salt and pepper, bring to the boil and simmer for around 45 minutes. Cool and strain the liquid. This will give you a pleasing, natural vegetable stock, for vegetarian soups, sauces, rice and pasta. It freezes well in small containers. Richer vegetable stocks may be made by frying the ingredients in a tablespoon or two of olive oil and using some mushrooms and a potato as well as the various vegetables listed above. If you don't want to make your own, you can find various brands of vegetable stock cubes and pastes, which I find very good, and they add oomph to pilaffs and sauces.

Fish Stock

Fish heads, tails, bones, remnants of sea food -- anything you can get! Simmered with chopped carrots, onions and celery and a light dusting of herbs and you have the basis for delicious fish soups and sauces. Freezes.

Mayonnaise

You will need a small food processor, unless you want to ruin your wrists whisking.

Ingredients
2 egg yolks
1 tbsp of vinegar or lemon juice
12.5 cl of salad oil
Salt and pepper

Method
*   Put the egg yolks, vinegar, salt and pepper into the mixer.
*   Dribble the oil slowly through the lid, while the mixer is running, until the right consistency is reached.

Aïoli

Cheats add some minced, pounded or powdered garlic to the above recipe, and this makes a perfectly acceptable sauce for slices of raw vegetables (*Crudités*). Purists make a sauce very similar to Skordalia (see page 29)

Or there is this simple recipe, found in France and Spain, for which you will need your small food processor, plus:
2 slices of white bread, crusts removed and whizzed into breadcrumbs. Then put in 3 garlic cloves and 6 tbsps. olive oil and whiz well. Finally 30 cl of mayonnaise and seasoning. Whiz again. Serve. Good.

Tartare Sauce the way Escoffier never made it *To accompany 6-8 portions of fish,*

On a chopping board, place:

1 very small cucumber, washed, topped and tailed
2 spring onions, washed
2 tsp pickled capers
1 sprig of parsley
2 small gherkins
6 or so pitted black olives

Mix everything together and chop finely.

Put the mixture into a ramekin and add 3 or 4 tbsp mayonnaise. Stir and sprinkle with a few separately chopped chives or sprig of parsley. I have to come clean and say that to the above agglomerate I like to add a teaspoon of mashed garlic.

Mostly a sauce like this goes on grilled or fried fish, but it also complements deep-fried battered mushrooms. It's not bad on its own with Pitta bread either!

Now I shall give you Escoffier's recipe for *La Vrai Sauce Tartare*. You will need 4-5 hard boiled egg yolks, salt and freshly ground pepper, 25 cl of oil, 1 teaspoon of vinegar, 2 tablespoons of mayonnaise and 1 tablespoon of chopped chives.

Sieve the egg yolks and pound into a paste with the salt and pepper. Then you slowly work in the oil, add the vinegar, and lastly the mayonnaise and chives. Watch out for curdling, or stick to my recipe!

Skordalia - Garlic Sauce

This is my version of an old Cyprus favourite that is beginning to re-appear on restaurant tables. Cypriots love Skordalia with beetroot (both fresh and canned are very good flavour and value), but it is splendid with grilled chicken and fried or grilled fish. Here again, a small food processor comes in very handy.

Ingredients

50g   [1 coffee cup] of blanched, peeled almonds
8 cl white wine vinegar
Half a piece of Pitta bread or 1 slice white bread, toasted
1 or 2 large cloves of garlic (according to taste)
10 cl of Sunflower oil
Salt and ground black pepper
10 cl of water or a little more

Method

*   Put almonds into food processor and whiz until ground.
*   Crumble bread and add to almonds. Whiz again.
*   Dribble in the vinegar - whiz. Dribble in the oil - whiz. (By now you should have a thick paste.)
*   Add salt and pepper - keep the whizzing going.
*   Slowly add the water until you get a lovely creamy, finger-licking good mixture.

It also makes a delicious "Dip" - slivers of carrot, cucumber, celery, goujons of fish on sticks, even potato flavoured crisps can be plonked in to fish out a spot of the noble garlic sauce.

Hilton Onion Marmalade

One lunch-time at the Nicosia Hilton, I ordered calves' liver with 'Hilton Onion Marmalade'. The liver was lovely, but I adored the "marmalade" and the then general manager, Ashley Spencer, obligingly provided the recipe. It goes well with liver, of course, but also with pork sausages, chops and fried fish.

Ingredients

300 g peeled onions, thinly sliced
5 cl corn or sunflower oil
100 g sugar
1 cinnamon stick
2-3 bay leaves
5-6 black peppercorns
5 cl white wine

Method

* In a medium frying pan, heat the oil and fry the onion.
* Add sugar, cinnamon, bay leaves and peppercorns.
* Continue frying until the onions are cooked to a golden colour and the sugar is caramelised.
* Add wine, to deglaze the pan.
* When cool, remove bay leaves and cinnamon stick.
* Serve cold.

Barbecue Sauce

You can use a proprietary brand if you wish, but it is cheaper and better to make your own and you can put in all the ingredients you like. Amongst the ones I use are: tomato purée, some vinegar and lemon, olive oil, garlic powder, a little chili pepper, a wee bit of sugar, soy sauce, sweet pepper sauce, wine, sherry, Worcestershire Sauce, ketchup and salt and pepper.

All you do is mix up your preferred barbecue sauce and schlap it over your meat, fish or vegetables, a little while before barbecuing.

Marinades

Marinading is the immersion of meat, fish or vegetables in a liquid mixture with a view to flavouring and/or tenderising them. The immersion may take minutes, hours, overnight or days. Yogurt is sometimes used, but the main ingredients are oil and an acid (vinegar, wine or lemon) to break down fibres and tenderise.

The basic marinade, to use with about one kilo of meat, fish or vegetables, comprises: 15 cl olive oil, 3 tbsp vinegar and/or lemon juice, 1 garlic clove, peeled and finely chopped, freshly ground black pepper and salt to taste. Thereafter, your imagination can run riot. For *red wine marinade,* use red wine vinegar in the basic recipe and add 1 cup of red wine, one small onion, peeled and finely chopped, chopped fresh thyme and a bay leaf. For *white wine marinade,* use white wine vinegar in the basic marinade and add a small sprig of rosemary and a sprig of thyme, finely chopped.

For some hotter stuff, *chili marinade* uses lemon juice instead of vinegar in the basic marinade, plus 3 tbsp tomato ketchup, a level tsp of paprika, a coffee spoon of powdered cumin, a pinch or two of dried oregano and sprinkles of chili pepper to the degree of hotness you require.

Mushroom Sauce

Ingredients *for 4-6 servings with grilled meat or fish, or Boeuf en Croute (see page 102)*

225 g of fresh button mushrooms, finely sliced
3 rashers of streaky bacon, cut into thin strips
1 medium carrot and 1 stalk celery, diced
1 des-sp flour
1 walnut sized knob of butter and 1 des-sp of olive oil
60 cl of beef stock (or boiling water and 1-2 beef stock cubes)
1-2 tsp tomato purée
4 tbsp Cyprus Muscat sweet white wine
Tiny sprinkling of chopped fresh herbs (thyme, sage, parsley)
Salt and pepper to taste

Method

* Heat the butter and oil in a shallow stewpan until bubbling.
* Put in the chopped bacon, carrot and celery and stir-fry on high heat until they start to brown at edges.
* Turn heat to medium and add the mushrooms. Cook for five minutes.
* Sprinkle over the flour and mix in. Cook gently for a minute or two, then stir in stock carefully.
* Add herbs, tomato purée and salt and pepper.
* Cover and simmer for 15-20 minutes.
* Remove sauce and put in a blender and whiz until smooth.

Before use/serving, heat the sauce gently, adding the Cyprus Muscat - but do *not* boil.

Mustard Sauce

This is really designed to be served with gravad lax, but it is also delicious with other marinaded fish, with smoked salmon, smoked trout and ham, hot or cold. It is also very good with slices of cold pork sausage.

Ingredients

2 tbsp of mixed mustard, preferably French or German.
(If you do not have this, powdered mustard and
half water and half vinegar to mix)
1 tbsp of caster sugar
2 tbsp of wine vinegar

1 egg yolk
7 tbs salad oil
1 tsp fresh or dried dill
Seasoning

Method

In a small bowl, beat with a small whisk the mustard, sugar and egg yolk.
Dribble in the oil and vinegar, whisking very well as you go. Sprinkle in the dill and seasoning, whisk again and serve.

This is a quick recipe but there is an even quicker one, which produces a very acceptable sauce in just a minute.

Quick Mustard Sauce

Ingredients

4 des-sps of mayonnaise
1 des-sp of salad oil
1 tsp of mustard powder

A pinch of black pepper
4 pinches of chopped dill
1 tsp of icing sugar (caster if you don't have icing)

Method

*   With a mini-whisk, blend everything together.

Remoulade Sauce

Ingredients

37.5 cl (half wine bottle) of mayonnaise
2 tbsp Dijon mustard
1 tbsp chopped gherkins

1 heaped tsp chopped capers
Pinch each of chopped parsley, chervil and tarragon
Half tsp anchovy essence

Method
Mix them all together.

Serve with fried fish, vegetables or cold meats

Tomato Sauce

This basic tomato sauce can be used for all kinds of dishes. It freezes well. It can be made in any quantity in the proportion of 1 onion to 3 tomatoes. These quantities will make enough to be going on with...

2-3 largish onions, peeled and finely chopped
6-8 large tomatoes, coarsely chopped
3-4 good cloves garlic, peeled and finely chopped
Sprig of thyme and several bay leaves
Salt and pepper
1-2 tbsp dry sherry
A little chili pepper if you want a hot touch
4-5 tbsp olive oil

Method
*   In a large heavy pot, heat the oil and fry onions and garlic until transparent.
*   Add herbs and the tomatoes.
*   Cover, stir well and cook on medium heat for 15-20 minutes, stirring from time to time.
*   Add sherry and seasonings. Simmer for 15 minutes.

If you want a thick sauce, remove the lid and simmer away liquid— watch out for burning, though! You can play about with the ingredients to your heart's content: more tomatoes, less onion, more garlic, no sherry (or *more* sherry), fresh herbs like basil, yummy! For a tomato coulis, remove mixture from pan and rub through a sieve or a Mouli. Chuck into food processor if you don't mind the pips. You can skin and de-seed the tomatoes before cooking if the seeds get into your teeth.

Ragu alla Bolognese

This is one of the world's classics. Mince. But doesn't **Ragu alla Bolognese** sound better? There are probably as many recipes for this as there are Italian Mamas and Chefs in Italian kitchens. This is one based on the recipe in a little Soho Italian spaghetti bar of the 1950's (Two Shillings a plate). As an impecunious young film publicist, it was home for me at lunch-hour about three times a week. It was one of the first Espresso bars in London, run by a chap called Claude Barnett and his wife, who, it was said had won £75,000 on Vernons Pools (a great deal of money then) with which they had set up the coffee bar, where Mrs Barnett cooked Spaghetti Bolgenese and Spaghetti Napoli every day. There were two notices, both salutary on the wall behind where a rather po-faced Claude presided over the Espresso machine. The first read: "In God we trust, others pay cash". The second: "If you're so clever, why aren't you rich?

Ingredients

450 g ground minced beef (or a mixture of beef, pork and veal)
2 medium onions and 1-2 cloves garlic, finely chopped
1 stick celery, 1 medium carrot, and a handful of dried or non-wet fresh mushrooms, finely chopped in a food processor
2 large tomatoes, skinned and chopped
Pinch of dried thyme, sage and 1 bay leaf
25 cl of red wine
Salt and Pepper
3 tbsp of olive oil

Method

* Into a heavy, large saucepan, put the olive oil and heat until it's moving about and looking hot.
* Put chopped onions and garlic into the pan and cook quickly, stirring frequently, until edges start to brown.
* Add ground meat and continue cooking on high heat, stirring a lot until meat starts to brown.
* Add minced celery/carrot/mushroom mixture, the herbs and the bay leaf, turn heat to medium and cook 5-10 . minutes stirring regularly.
* Put in the chopped tomatoes, stir briskly and add the wine.

* Put lid on pan and cook on low heat. After 15 minutes or so, check liquid level. A drop more wine, or water, may be needed.
* Simmer slowly for an hour or so, checking from time to time and loooking at liquid level, till it looks right, smells right and tastes right.

Like every basic recipe, people all over the world vary the ingredients. Some add some chicken livers, bacon or ham, to the meat mixture, others (like me) balance the weight of meat to an equal weight of the vegetables. But whatever you do, you have the basic sauce for any boiled pasta, for lasagne, risotto and a host of other meals. One thing I do regard as essential: a good olive oil for the cooking. Fat, butter or light oils just won't do.

Ragu freezes perfectly. Once a month, I make up a large potful and decant it into 15 - 20 two-portion terra cotta yogurt pots (the yogurt formerly in said pots is good, too) and then freeze it. Once a week, or so, when we're too tired to cook or even go out, out comes a pot, on goes the pasta and Presto!, a meal. A little salad on the side, a cheerful young, fruity red wine, and some smoked fish to start, what better?

Rich Red Tomato Chutney

Sometimes, one is faced with a pile of very ripe tomatoes. You can simply wash them, bag 'em and freeze 'em. Otherwise you can make a fruity chutney, to serve with cold meats, as a topping to toasted cheese, or alongside a curry.

Ingredients

1 k of ripe tomatoes, skinned
500 g of firm onions, peeled
250 g of unsweet apples, peeled and cored
750 g pitted raisins and sultanas mixed
250 g soft brown sugar
60 cl of white wine vinegar
Flavourings (see below)

Method

* Chop the onions, apples and tomatoes quite finely
* In a large heavy pot, put all ingredients and bring to the boil.
* Add flavourings of your choice, e.g. ground ginger, a pinch of allspice, ground cloves or cumin. If you want an oriental flavour, add cumin, turmeric and a pinch or two of chili pepper.
* Simmer until you have a nice thick gooey texture—at least one hour.
* Cool and ladle into clean jam jars. You'll get at least three jars depending on the size of jar.

Sauces using Milk and Cream

White Sauce

The basis of many good dishes. It is simply flour, butter and milk. You use butter and flour in equal measures.

* Put a good knob of butter (about ⅛th of a 225g packet) into a small-to-medium heavy pan and gently melt it. Sprinkle in a little flour and mix. When it is mixed, if there is butter still running, put in a little more flour and mix again over a low heat until you have a nice, floury, buttery ball.

* Remove the pan from the heat and put in a little milk. With a wooden spoon, mix the milk into the ball until it is entirely absorbed. Stir this over a low heat for a minute or two.

* Remove the pan and repeat the operation: pour in more milk, mix the ball, until you have a very thick, smooth sauce. Put back on the burner, keep stirring and cooking.

* Remove again, add more milk, blend with your spoon and cook again. Do this until you have the consistency of sauce that you want.

* Add salt and pepper to taste, and anything else you want: bits of bacon, bits of cheese, herbs or whatever you want to flavour your sauce.

Using a Roux (other than Michel and Albert)

The flour-butter ball is a very useful agent for thickening soups and stews. A small one, for example, dropped into a pan of vegetable soup and stirred until it is dissolved will provide a gentle thickening, whilst a larger one will delightfully thicken a vegetable stew or casserole of, say, celery, onions and carrots in vegetable stock.

Simple Saucifying

A simple way to make, let us say, an onion sauce or a mushroom sauce is as follows.

Fry onions or mushrooms in a reasonable quantity of oil and/or butter and when they are nearly cooked, sprinkle over a spoon or so of flour. Stir this in and cook for a minute or two, taking care not to burn.

Then slowly pour in, mixing as you go, milk/stock/wine or other liquid. Gently cook this, stirring all the time – and presto – you have a very quick sauce.

Bechamel Sauce

You see this in loads of recipes and there are lots and lots of variations. Basically, it is flavoured white sauce.

One Italian variation is to chop finely a little onion, a little celery and a little bacon and to put this in milk which is slowly heated almost to boiling point. This flavoured milk is then used to make the sauce as above. Another "infusion" into the milk is half a small bay leaf, a very small onion and a sprig of herb such as thyme. The flavoured milk should be passed through a sieve when making the sauce, unless you want bits of herb or bacon mixture in the sauce, which frankly I don't mind at all.

Cream

How many thousands of restaurants take the ultimate short cut and just run a little cream into a dish like escalope of chicken or veal just as it comes to completion? It's a rich but quick and very delicious way of saucing your dish. Just put in the cream, stir carefully over not too high a heat and blend with the juices in the pan just before serving.

Egg and Parsley Sauce

Ingredients

2 hard-boiled eggs (ten minute jobs)
1 tbsp lemon juice
2 sprigs parsley, very finely chopped
2 egg whites

1 tsp sunflower oil
Salt and pepper
1 tbsp cream

Method

* Cut eggs in half and remove yolks.
* In a bowl, mix yolks with oil
* Add a little salt, a sprinkle of pepper, parsley and lemon juice.
* In a food processor or with a whisk beat egg whites until stiff.
* Fold egg whites into yolk mixture and mix in the cream. Serve.

Lovely. And what can you do with the two spare egg yolks? Some home-made mayonnaise or Aïoli. (see page 27)

Herb Sauce

Ingredients
15 cl of mayonnaise
15 cl of sheep's yogurt
2 hard-boiled egg yolks
1 teaspoon of made mustard, preferably Dijon; or, if you don't have this, Colman's
1 tablespoon of chopped fresh dill
1 tablespoon of chopped chives or very finely chopped green salad onion
1 tablespoon of chopped parsley
Salt and pepper

Method
* In a bowl, blend the mayonnaise and yogurt.
* In another bowl, mash the egg yolks and the mustard and stir the yogurt/mayonnaise into them.
* Add salt and pepper to taste.
* Stir in the chopped herbs.

And what can you do with this? All sorts of things. You can make a Kohl-rabi Salad as an hors d'oeuvres dish, for example. You will need a couple of smallish kohl-rabi, which you peel very carefully and then either grate or chop into very small juliennes. Mix the herb sauce into this and it is very tasty indeed. The sauce also makes a good addition to the meze table, amongst the tahini, hommous etc. I have to admit that I like to dip potato crisps into it!

Soups, starters and Mezedes

Soups, Starters and Mezedes

Gazpacho

I first encountered this lovely cold soup in a shaded discreet restaurant in Madrid, where my host, familiar with the recipe, was eyeing two elegant married ladies dining at an adjoining table; the local sport, he said. Being of a slightly cautious disposition, I preferred to eye the soup.

Ingredients *for 4 people*

750 g of peeled tomatoes
1 medium Cyprus cucumber, peeled
About 60 g of "old" bread (1 good slice)
30 cl of water
Salt and pepper

1 large or 2 small green peppers, destalked and deseeded
1 large clove of garlic, peeled and sliced
15 cl of olive or sunflower oil
4 tbsps white wine vinegar

Method
* Crumble the bread into a dish and pour over vinegar, to soak for 5-10 minutes.
* Coarsely chop tomatoes, peppers and cucumber. Blend with the bread and garlic in a food processor until smooth.
* Gradually add the oil, continuing blending.
* Slowly add the water and blend until creamily "soupy", adding more water if necessary.
* Taste and add salt and pepper to taste. Sometimes a little more vinegar gives further bite.
* Pour into a bowl, cover and leave in the fridge for at least 6 hours.

Borscht

Ingredients

1 litre of chicken stock	500 g of uncooked beetroot
1 large onion	1 large potato
1 carrot and 1 stick celery	1 level tbsp tomato purée
Salt and black pepper	1 small carton of sour cream
One good knob of butter	

Method

*   Wash, peel and dice the beetroot, potato and carrot.
*   Peel and chop the onion very finely and slice the celery stalk very thinly.
*   In a large pot melt the butter and put in all the vegetables. Cover and cook on a medium heat for around 5 minutes stirring from time to time.
*   Add the stock, tomato purée, salt and pepper, stir and bring to the boil.
*   Cover and simmer for about 50 minutes.
*   Put the soup into a blender and whiz for a few seconds (not too long—it's not a cream soup!)
*   Serve hot in bowls, into which a nice dollop of sour cream is swirled. Sprinkle some chopped chives or a little chopped parsley on the top.

If you like, you may impart an additional sweet-sour flavour by adding a little sugar during cooking and at the end the juice of half a lemon. A ham stock can be used instead of chicken ... and so on... The variations of Borscht are many. What to drink with Borscht? Russians and Poles like alternate spoonfuls of soup and swigs of Vodka and I must admit I find this very enjoyable. Nevertheless, a couple of plates of Borscht with Vodka accompaniment are, for me at any rate, a recipe for falling over!

Cream of Asparagus Soup -- 4-6 servings

Ingredients
1 standard bundle of Cyprus asparagus (about 450 g)
1 medium onion
2 small to medium potatoes
50 cl chicken or vegetable stock and 50 cl milk
Salt and pepper to taste
Butter

Method

* Wash the asparagus, cut the woody bits from the bottom of the stems and, with a sharp knife, scrape very well the lower parts to remove the stringy bits.
* Slice the asparagus into slivers. Set aside the flowers at the top, which you must cook separately.
* Peel and cut the potatoes into small sections, and peel and slice the onion finely.
* In a heavy pan, melt 2 good knobs of butter and stir-fry for a few minutes the potatoes, the onion and all the asparagus except the flowers.
* Pour in the stock/milk. Bring carefully to the boil, cover and simmer for 15-20 minutes or until the asparagus is well cooked through.
* In a separate small pan gently simmer the flowery tops of the asparagus until they are not quite cooked through. Drain and set aside.
* Drain the liquid from the large pan into a bowl and then put the cooked asparagus, potato and onion into a food-processor and purée thoroughly. Return the purée and the liquid to the big pan and whisk, adding salt and pepper to taste.
* Chop the tops of the asparagus quite finely and, just before serving, mix into the soup.
* Ladle into bowls, add a swirl of cream and a little sprinkling of parsley or chives, and serve at once.

Note: you have to be careful to avoid stringy asparagus. If you cook the stringy stuff you may have to put the soup through a Mouli. The soup may be thickened by increasing the quantity of potato. It is also delicious cold, and makes a variation of Vichyssoise, especially if you chop plenty of chives into the soup as you serve it.

A trio of simple Soups..

Pea

Good soup is so simple when you have a litre or two of stock. This pea soup is excellent. Chop a medium onion finely and fry in a knob of butter until starting to brown. Throw in 450 g of frozen peas, stir round, cover and cook for five minutes. Add a litre of stock, bring to boil and simmer until peas are tender. Whizz in a blender until creamy. Serve with a swirl of cream and some *croutons* (which you made earlier) in each bowl and some green decoration on top (chives, parsley or mint).

Ham and Pea: just chop some bacon, ham or lounza finely and fry with the onion, as for pea soup.

Creamy Broad Bean

Fry a chopped onion in butter. Add a rasher or two of bacon and fry for a few minutes. Add a litre of a good light meat or chicken stock. Bring to the boil. Add half a kilo of skinned broad beans and simmer until they are cooked through. With a slotted spoon take out all solids and put into a food processor and whizz until smooth. Return to the pan and stir.
Serve into soup bowls and stir in to each one a tablespoon of cream. Sprinkle with croutons and a little chopped parsley and serve at once with a glass of dry sherry or Sercial Madeira.

Cream adds a certain something to many soups, but is superfluous (or should I say SOUPerfluous?) with one of my all-time favourites, which, like so many recipes can be varied according to what's available in the market or your larder, and it's next...

Minestrone

Ingredients *for 4-6 plates*

2 medium onions, 2 carrots, 1 stick celery, finely chopped
3 rashers streaky bacon, diced
A handful of button mushrooms, chopped
2 cabbage leaves, finely chopped

2 tomatoes, peeled and chopped
155 g of rice-shaped pasta ("Kritharaki")
1 l of chicken stock
Butter for frying
Salt and pepper to taste

Method

* Melt butter in a large pan. Add chopped bacon and fry until starting to brown.
* Put in the chopped onions, carrots, celery, mushrooms and cabbage leaves.
* Put lid on pan and cook over medium heat for five minutes stirring regularly.
* Add tomatoes, stir and cook for a few minutes more.
* Add stock, bring to boil and simmer for about 15 minutes.
* Put in the pasta, bring back to boil and simmer until it is tender.

Serve with grated Parmesan cheese and plenty of hot, fresh bread.

You can permutate ingredients happily: different pasta, rice instead of pasta, some diced potato, turnip, swede... and so on, according to what's in your cupboards.

Potage Paysanne

A sturdy soup for colder days. It can use a variety of vegetables, according to availability.

Ingredients (4-6 *plates*)

150 g butter
2-3 sticks celery, finely sliced.
2 smallish leeks and 1 medium onion
  (or 2 largish onions) finely chopped
3 rashers streaky bacon, cut into thin slivers
1 tbsp flour
75 cl of hot chicken or light meat stock

2 large carrots, 2 small turnips and 2 small parsnips,
  finely diced, or an equal volume of any root vegetables
  (except beetroot)
150 g mushrooms, finely chopped
3 medium tomatoes, skinned and de-seeded.
12.5 cl milk

Method

*   Melt butter in a large thick saucepan.
*   Fry leek/onion, bacon, mushrooms and celery for around 5 minutes stirring regularly.
*   Add root vegetables, stir and cook on medium heat for around five minutes, stirring now and then.
*   Remove pan from cooker, stir in flour and cook gently for a couple of minutes, stirring the while.
*   Add milk, stir in carefully, and cook a minute or two.
*   Add tomatoes and stock, slowly, stirring carefully.
*   Bring slowly to boil, turn down heat and simmer for around 30 minutes.

If you like thick soup, use a little more flour. If you like it thinner, add more stock at the simmering point.
Serve with croutons, if you like, and sprinkle mint and parsley about with gay abandon if you choose, but for me some crunchy, crispy fresh baked village bread is the only accompaniment necessary.

Asparagus

The sight of a road-side stall near Episkopi, with the most beautiful plump and flavoursome strawberries, together with bundles of the freshest asparagus, reminds one of a good English summer, and they do make the important components of a lovely meal. And the season seems to get longer and longer!

There are many things you can do with asparagus, but let's start simply by boiling it.

* Cut any choggy or woody bits from the bottom of the asparagus.
* With a sharp knife, scrape the bottom section of the stem to remove the stringy bits.
* Tie or put an elastic band around the asparagus to make a bundle.
* If you have a very deep pot, stand the bundles of asparagus in it and fill with water half way up the bundles. If you don't, but you have a very large frying or sauté pan, lay some forks or something similar on one side and set the bundles down so that the tips of the asparagus are clear of the water.
* Cover your pan, bring the water to the boil and cook on a moderate heat for about 10-12 minutes.

Serve hot with melted butter, or cold with French dressing or mayonnaise.

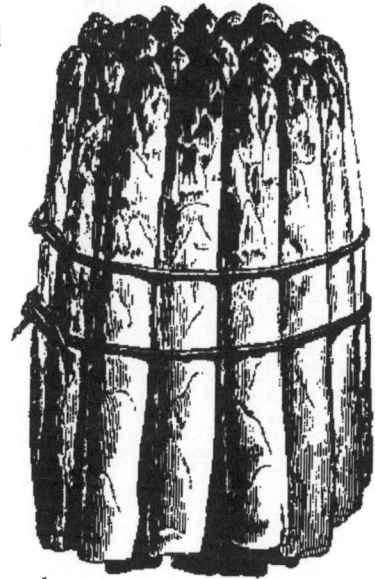

Asparagus and Prawn Salad
An Hors d'Oeuvre or buffet dish.

Ingredients, *to serve 6-8*

2 bundles of asparagus
4 hard-boiled eggs
Mayonnaise

1 cup of cooked North Atlantic Prawns
2-3 medium tomatoes, skins removed
Vinaigrette
1 tbsp mayonnaise

Method

* Chop the prawns and mix with mayonnaise.
* Cook the asparagus as outlined on the previous page.
* Hard boil the eggs for 10-12 minutes, drain and plunge straight into cold water.
* On a large serving platter, arrange the cooked asparagus in an artistic fashion.
* Peel and halve the hard-boiled eggs, remove the yolks and combine them with the prawn mixture.
* Stuff the halved egg whites with the prawn/egg yolk mixture.
* Slice the tomatoes and place in between or around the asparagus; then complete the display by adding the halved, stuffed eggs.
* With your maximum artistry, dot some mayonnaise, topped by a tiny bit of parsley, on the asparagus and serve well chilled.

To accompany: a fruity white wine.

Alison's Country Terrine

Food author Alison and her sister Kate ran a very good restaurant in Kent with a pretty eclectic menu. One night, sampling a delicious paté maison, I asked Alison the ingredients. She looked round the crowded room, bent over and whispered in my ear: "Pig's liver and pork sausage meat". It's a good and inexpensive combination.

Ingredients *for a Paté terrine or 30 cm long bread/cake tin. This will make 12-15 good slices.*

225 g streaky bacon
450 g of pork sausage meat
1 onion and 2-3 garlic cloves, finely chopped
Pinch of thyme and sage, half tsp powdered ginger
Salt and pepper

450 g pig's liver
150 g of Cyprus lounza, ham or bacon, chopped
1 egg, beaten
1 tbsp dry sherry or brandy

Method

* Heat oven to 180 °C   Line the terrine dish, or tin with the streaky bacon.
* Mince or blend quickly the liver. Transfer to a large mixing bowl.
* Add all the other ingredients and mix well with a wooden spoon.
* Transfer the mixture to the bacon-lined terrine and cover tightly with aluminium foil. Put a heavy lid on top.
* Fill a large baking tray half way up with water and stand the terrine in it.
* Place the tray in the centre of a medium oven and cook for about one and half hours.
* Remove from the oven, take off lid and put a heavy weight on top of the foil (I use a clean brick) and leave to cool.
* When cool, you may remove the foil, decorate the top with bay leaves, thin slivers of red pepper and some peppercorns or juniper berries. Then dribble over a little warmed thick stock or aspic which will cool and jellify.

Blender Smoked Haddock Paté

Ingredients

650 g of Smoked Haddock fillet
1 small carton of double cream
50 g butter
2 tsp lemon juice and 1 tsp of Worcester sauce
Salt and black pepper

Method
* Poach the haddock fillet in milk until flaky. Remove the skin. Discard the milk, or give to the cat.
* Flake the haddock and put into a food processor with the butter.
* Add the cream—blend. Add the lemon juice and Worcester Sauce—blend. Season to taste, adding a pinch of ground red or Cayenne pepper if you like it a little hot.
* Spoon into a small bowl or six ramekins.
* Melt a couple of good knobs of butter and pour over the top of the bowl or ramekins.
* Refrigerate for 2-3 hours before serving. Keeps for several days.

An alternative is to delete the cream and use only butter -- in which case you should put in 300 grams.

Fino Liver Paté

Ingredients -- *for 6-8 servings as a starter*

250 g of chicken livers
1 medium onion, finely chopped
A good handful of button mushrooms, sliced
3 rashers of bacon or slices of lounza
100 g butter
Pinch of fresh thyme, 1 coffee spoon dried ginger, a pinch of allspice, salt and pepper
2 tbsp KEO "FINO" (dry Cyprus sherry)

Method

* Trim all fat and gristle away from the chicken livers. If the chicken hearts are attached, let them be, they will add to the flavour. Slice coarsely.
* In a medium frying-pan, heat 30 grams of the butter until sizzling and add the onions, the bacon, herbs, spices and mushrooms. Cook until beginning to turn brown. Remove and put into your food processor.
* Put another 30 g of butter into the pan and fry the livers for around 5 minutes until cooked through ("pinky"), remove, and put into the food processor.
* Put remaining butter and sherry, salt and pepper, into food processor and whiz until smooth and creamy.
* Spoon into a medium bowl or individual ramekins. Refrigerate for at least three hours.

Serve with "Fino", or a very dry white wine.

Fish Paté This is very pleasant as a starter, especially if you make a little *coulis* to go with it.

Ingredients

450 g of red snapper fillet, skin removed
250 g of unsalted butter (soft)
125 g of bread crumbs (home made) which you have moistened with 30 ml of cream
2 egg yolks, beaten
2 tbsp of finely chopped parsley

2 tbsp of fresh finely chopped dill or 1 tbsp of dried dill
2 salad onions, finely chopped
450 g of salmon fillet, which has been marinaded for an hour or two in dry white wine, salt and a sprinkling of mace or allspice
Salt and pepper

Method

* Marinade salmon
* Heat the oven to 175°C
* Chop the red snapper fillets into pieces and mince very finely, two or three times if necessary. Put in a bowl.
* Mix into the fish the soft unsalted butter.
* In another bowl, put the cream-moistened bread crumbs and the 2 beaten egg yolks. Mix well.
* Add the finely chopped parsley, the finely chopped salad onions, the dill, a little salt and pepper and mix well.
* Add the fish mixture and beat everything together until it is lovely and light and quite fluffy.
* Thoroughly butter the inside of a medium paté terrine and put a layer of the fish mixture on the bottom.
* Then put a layer of the marinaded salmon, and finally a layer of the red snapper mixture. Cover the top with soft butter, dabbed well over.
* Seal with aluminium foil and, if the terrine has a lid, put it on the top.
* Put the terrine in a large oven dish and pour boiling water into the oven dish until it is half way up the terrine.
* Bake in a medium oven, 175 Centigrade, for about 2 hours.

Serve hot with hollandaise sauce or a tomato *coulis*. (Foot of page 35) It may also be served cold, with mayonnaise.

Mezedes

The sight of a meze table fully set is an inspiring one. "How on earth have they done all that?" you ask yourself; but if you look, on closer inspection a lot of the little dishes have come out of jars, cans, packets and the freezer. And you can produce a wonderful table as a buffet, hors d'oeuvres or simply for people to pick and choose. I would also recommend you look at the section on salads (pages 153 to 164). Several of these dishes are ideal for the meze table, particularly Tabbouleh and Fattoush. Produce a selection from this little lot and wait for the "Ooohs" and "Aaahs".

* Pork chipolata sausages, simply baked in a hot oven for around 20 minutes, cut in half and speared with cocktail sticks.
* Pieces of canned asparagus rolled in a slice of ham.
* Small cheese biscuits spread with Scandinavian Cods' Roe paste (e.g. Kavli "Kaviar", widely available), topped with a slice of gherkin or olive.
* Frozen mini vol-aux-vents, baked and filled with anything suspended in a white/cheese sauce, such as fried chopped mushrooms, tiny pieces of cooked chicken, bolognese sauce, chopped asparagus, prawns or chopped crab sticks.
* Goujons of fried fish, such as frozen red mullet fillets, defrosted, sliced into strips, dipped in flour, then beaten egg and fried in hot oil. These can be prepared beforehand and warmed.
* Cheesy, fish, creamy or yogurty dips for tasting on crisps, tortillas, strips of carrot or cucumber.
* Grilled loukanika, or other spiced sausage, sliced and speared with cocktail sticks.
* Grilled halloumi and lounza slices.
* Canned smoked oysters, wrapped in a bacon rasher and grilled.
* Dishes of green and black olives
* Hiromeri, Parma ham or similar and melon
* Large defrosted prawns, quickly turned in very hot olive oil, garlic and a squirt of Tabasco
* Little kalamares fried in egg and flour

Aubergine & Tahini Purée

This is a great favourite throughout the Middle East and the Eastern Mediterranean. It is easy to make (though in restaurants all too often carelessly done -- the slightly burnt flavour must come through). In Greek it is called Melitzanasalata, in Lebanon Br'tinjan bi Tahini and in Egypt Baba Ghanouch. Whatever it is called it makes a delicious starter with hot Arabic or Pitta bread, especially as part of a Meze or Hors d'Hoeuvres. Toasted pine seeds make an exotic topping.

*   Put two medium aubergines under a hot grill, until one side is quite burnt (about 8 minutes). Turn over and do the other side.
*   Remove from grill, leave to cool a little, then cut in half and scoop all the cooked flesh out, including some of the toasted skin (a slightly burnt flavour adds to the effect).
*   In your food processor, put the aubergine flesh, two/three tbsp of tahini paste, some cloves of garlic, 1 tbsp lemon juice, salt and pepper and whiz until you have got a lovely smooth paste.
*   Put into a bowl, pat the top with a fork, dribble some olive oil round the edge and put a sprig of parsley in the middle.

Tsatsiki

Tsatsiki, a.k.a. Talatouri, is simply a mixture of yogurt, peeled and finely chopped cucumber, finely chopped or pulverised garlic, mint, salt and pepper. You can add some very finely sliced onion, chives or garlic chives if you like. Tsatsiki is lovely with grilled meat, especially lamb and with spiced chicken and rice.

Felafel

One of the great dishes-of-the-people of the Middle East, nowhere better than from street stalls in Cairo. A wonderful meat substitute and backbone of a fine Arabian vegetarian meal.

Ingredients for 4, servings or as part of a buffet menu
500 g of dried broad beans.
2 medium sized onions and 1 large clove garlic
1 tsp ground coriander seeds

1 tsp ground cumin
2 pinches of baking powder
2-3 sprigs parsley
Salt and freshly ground pepper

Method

* 24 hours before you make the Felafel, soak the beans.
* Remove the beans from the water, place on a wire rack and leave to dry. Pat with a cloth if necessary to remove all the water.
* In a mortar, pound the beans to a paste or *thoroughly* mince them in an electric blender. Remove and put into a bowl.
* Chop the onion, garlic and parsley very finely.
* Put all the ingredients, including the baking powder, spices and seasoning into a blender and whiz into as fine a paste mixture as you can.
* Remove, knead, and let the mixture stand in fridge for 30-45 minutes.
* When you're ready to cook, take a des-sp of the mixture, compress it in your hand and shape into a flat "burger". The mixture should make between 12 and 20 according to how big you make each one. Set aside for 15 minutes.
* In a deep frying pan or skillet heat around half a litre of sunflower oil.

Continued on next page.

*   Put the Felafel one by one onto a metal slotted spoon and slide into the hot oil. Fry until each one is crispy and golden all over.

*   Remove from the oil, pat dry on kitchen paper and serve at once, with tomato or mixed salad, some tahinisalata or yogurt.

Sometimes, if the mixture is not ground finely enough, it may not bind together well, but with a little practice, perfect Felafel can be made every time—and home-made are better than packet mixtures or deep-frozen ones! In some countries, chick-peas are substituted for dried broad beans — and a can of these, drained, can help you make a variety of Felafel very quickly.

Hommous

Ingredients

1 400 g can or jar of Chick Peas
2 tbsp of Tahini paste

2-3 medium-sized cloves of garlic
Juice of 1 lemon (more if you like)
2 tbsp of sunflower oil
Salt and pepper

Method
*   Drain the liquid from the chick peas and set aside.
*   Put the chick peas in your food processor/blender.
*   Add the tahini, garlic cloves, lemon juice and sunflower oil, and blend.
*   Season to taste and add as much of the chick pea liquid as you want to produce a creamy, not-too-runny 'dip'.

Dried chick peas need a good soak and a long cook, but if you do use the dried variety remember they never actually get totally soft, no matter how long you cook them. I use canned or bottled, because the liquid greatly helps the flavour of the dish.

Bruschetta (Garlic Toast)

For this Italian recipe, eight thick slices of fresh crusty Village bread are required. Alternatively, you could also use French bread cut in half lengthways. You will also need 2-3 cloves of garlic and a cup of olive oil.

Method

*   Heat oven to 200°C.
*   Put the sliced bread on a rack in the oven and leave it till it is crisp and gold on both sides.
*   Peel the garlic and crush, leaving the cloves whole.
*   Rub the garlic well and truly all over the hot toasted bread.
*   Sprinkle bread with plenty of salt and pepper and brush the olive oil over both sides.
*   Keep in a warm oven until ready to serve.

To serve with what? Cured meats, raw sliced vegetables, tahini, hommous, taramasalata, aïoli and with main dishes such as herby grilled fish, charcoal grilled steaks, green salad...

Crostini

A variation on the Bruscetta theme. Crostini is, are, oiled or buttered-on-both-sides slices of bread, which are fried or baked.

They form a simple and inexpensive platform for lots of snacky dishes or something substantial for that all-too-often indigestion-creating event the "finger buffet". Prepared in advance, a few minutes in a hot oven creates lovely warm "Antipasti".

*   Chicken liver paté is one good topping. (See page 55 for recipe)
*   Sliced sautéd mushrooms are another.
*   Then there is sliced cheese (of the melting variety such as Mozzarella or Tilsit), two canned anchovy fillets and a slice of tomato atop each toast. Bake till cheese melts.
*   You can top toast with cooked prawns, grate cheese over and bake or put under a hot grill for a minute or two.
*   Or a pizza topping, especially vegetarian varieties.

Garlic Pitta

*   Slice open the Pitta bread.
*   Brush the inside with a little olive oil.
*   Rub a garlic clove over the oiled bread. Or if you are a garlic fanatic, scatter finely chopped garlic inside the Pitta.
*   Close and put under a very hot grill for not more than 1 minute each side.

Pasta

Pasta and other Farinaceous Dishes

Pasta and other Farinaceous dishes

I love fresh bread – French baguettes, pitta, crusty loaves, Scottish farmhouse baps. I love pancakes, be they Mexican tortillas or Shrove Tuesday variety, but above all, of the products made with flour, pasta is my thing.

The day I graduated from canned spaghetti to the Italian variety was a turning point in my life. Spaghetti is still my favourite, but I love tagliatelli; I love the little kritharaki, the Cyprus barley-shaped tiny pasta; I love Thai noodles. And the beauty of all this is that you can put a sauce or a topping that is so quick and so simple it just isn't true.

With a good half kilo of ragu (page 36) you can make Spaghetti Bolognese; or use it for any variety of pasta shell, pasta quill of your choice. You can take a packet (454g) of lasagne pasta, boil it up (or use pre-cooked) and layer it with said ragu and top it off with a white sauce (page 39). Top it with grated cheese and put in a very hot oven for a few minutes. Lovely.

You can make beautiful pasta sauces with onions, tomato, garlic and cooked fish of your choice, with a few prawns and mussels thrown in for good measure.

Wherever you are you have access to a wide variety of Italian spaghetti. The Cyprus food industry has come a long way in recent years, and now makes, to my mind, many varieties of first class pasta. There is a greater range of locally made and imported pasta here than ever before and the sheer variety provides a cook with enormous incentive. Such is the range and the quality that making your own is too much fuff. I always return to my basic love—spaghetti, because I enjoy the twirling of it on the fork and the texture of the pasta itself.

Simply Spaghetti

You can put almost any sauce on spaghetti, including decidedly Chinese stir-fries and some very exotic Italian ones. Or you can keep it quick, simple and cheap.

Let's start by boiling a packet (450 g) of normal thickness pasta in a large pot of salted water. It takes from 10 to 12 minutes and should still have a little "bone" in it ("al dente") You drain it and put into a large lightly oiled or buttered bowl. And NOW... How do I serve thee? Let me count the ways... All quantities based on using 450 g of pasta, which serves 4-6.

Just Buttery

Flake some chilled unsalted butter and mix it in the pasta—superb as it is. Add some grated Parmesan or other hard cheese if you will.

Aglio e Olio (Garlic and oil) .

Ingredients
5 tbsp olive oil
5 cloves of garlic, peeled
Several sprigs of parsley, chopped
Salt and ground black pepper

* Mince or finely chop the garlic. Heat the oil and fry the garlic until it is golden brown.
* Remove garlic and keep the oil warm.
* Drain your perfectly cooked pasta and put in a large warmed bowl. Grind some black pepper over it, add the warm oil and stir in. Lastly, sprinkle over the chopped parsley.

There are many who like this dish peppery hot and this is done by frying a small red chili pepper along with the garlic and discarding it at the same time.

The Classics

Bolognese

The meat sauce recipe, "Ragu" is on page 36   Although not acknowledged in its native country as a two-some, Spaghetti Bolognese has virtually conquered the world. Ragu is splendid, too, with green or white tagliatelle, spooned over vegetable ravioli, on gnocchi, risotto and lots, lots more.

Napolitana

Perhaps even more versatile than Ragu, the Italian tomato sauce (page 35) not only accompanies pasta and rice, but meat, fish and vegetables. And it's *good for you.*

Arrabiata (the hot one)   Ingredients for four servings

350 g ridged penne or other large quill pasta
1 medium onion, peeled and sliced
1 good clove of garlic peeled and finely chopped
115 g of streaky bacon finely sliced

500 g ripe tomatoes, peeled and chopped
1 fresh red chili pepper.
2 tbsp grated hard cheese (Pecorino or Kefalotiri)
1 tbsp butter

* Heat butter and fry onion and garlic, till golden.
* Add tomatoes and chili pepper, simmer for 15 mins.
* Discard chili pepper when sauce is "hot" enough.
* Cook pasta in lots of boiling water for about 8 mins

* Drain most of water and add grated cheese to pasta.
* Cook gently for about 5 minutes, stirring regularly.
* Add more liquid if necessary to keep juicy.
* Serve with more grated cheese on top.

Spaghetti with Fresh Tomatoes

This spaghetti recipe is notable for the absence of a cooked sauce, but a few hours for marinading are required.

Ingredients for 4 portions

6 medium-sized tomatoes, carefully skinned, choggy bits removed and chopped
6 tbsp of best olive oil
Several sprigs of fresh basil
1 large garlic clove, crushed

Method

* Put the chopped tomatoes into a large bowl.
* Tear the basil leaves into small pieces and add to the tomatoes with the crushed garlic clove.
* Pour over the olive oil, stir, cover the bowl with a cloth and leave to stand in a cool place (not in the fridge) for at least eight hours.
* When mealtime is nigh, cook medium thickness spaghetti in a large pot of boiling salted water, 85-100 g per person, until softish but still with a bit of body ("*al dente*").
* Drain the spaghetti and put into a big warmed bowl.
* Pour over the tomato sauce, stir and cover.
* Serve after five minutes, with grated dry cheese if desired.

Pasta with Black Olives & Cyprus Capers

A sauce you can make hours or even a day beforehand

Ingredients
24 large black olives, pitted and cut into quarters
1 small can tomato purée
1 heaped tbsp of thoroughly drained Cyprus capers
1 red chili pepper, de-seeded

Method
*   Chop the drained capers finely and put in a small bowl with the quartered olives, the de-seeded chili pepper and the oil.
*   Add tomato purée and mix to quite a smooth sauce.

When you have your hot cooked pasta and you are ready to serve, remove the chili from the sauce. Mix the sauce into the pasta and serve, with green salad and hot bread.

Pasta with Peas and Mushrooms

Ingredients
600 g fresh button mushrooms, sliced
100 g streaky bacon, diced
500 g of frozen green peas
50 g butter

Method
* Melt the butter in a thick, medium-sized saucepan and sauté the bacon, peas and mushrooms together for about 15 minutes, or until the peas are done. Season to taste.
* Pour over the hot cooked pasta and serve with grated hard cheese.

Tomato & Black Olive Pasta Sauce

A *cold sauce, made of*

2-4 ripe, peeled, de-seeded, chopped tomatoes
A cup of pitted, chopped, black olives
Small torn pieces of fresh basil leaves
2 tbsp olive oil
1-2 tsp lemon juice
Salt and pepper

This is a very pleasant summer sauce, which you can serve with hot or cold pasta, or risotto. An Italian friend "shows" the chopped tomatoes to a few tablespoons of very hot olive oil in a frying pan for about 30 seconds, which imparts a lovely flavour.

She then adds the other ingredients and serves immediately.

Spaghetti con le Polpettine (Spaghetti and Meatballs)

Ingredients

1 medium sized onion, finely chopped
2 cloves garlic finely chopped
170 g lean pork, finely ground
170 g lean beef, finely ground
2 eggs
Tomato Sauce (See recipe on page 35)

2 sprigs of parsley, chopped
2 slices of white bread, crusts removed
2 tbsp grated Parmesan cheese
Salt and pepper

Method

* In your frying pan heat 2 tbsp of olive oil and fry the onions and garlic until golden
* Remove, leaving as much oil as possible in the pan.
* In a large bowl, put the onions and garlic and mix in all the other ingredients very well.
* Make the mixture into nice small meatballs about 3 cm across. Roll them in flour and quickly brown them in hot oil (add more of this if necessary).
* When browned, remove the meatballs and put them into a large pan of tomato sauce (which you made earlier). and simmer for 15-20 minutes.
* In a large pan, cook a packet of spaghetti in loads of boiling salted water. When nicely chewy, drain, put in a large serving dish and pour the meatballs and tomato sauce over.

Serve with grated Parmesan and a green salad. A fairly light fruity red wine to accompany. .

Pasta Pilaffi

This uses small barley-shaped pasta called 'Kritharaki' in Cyprus

Ingredients for 4 servings

225 g of button mushrooms, thinly sliced
1 medium onion, peeled and thinly sliced
1 clove of garlic, finely chopped (optional)
Half a glass of dry white wine

Salt and pepper
350 g of Kritharaki
At least 1 l of chicken stock, or water and 2 stock cubes

Method

* In a frying pan melt a good sized blob of butter until sizzling.
* Fry the sliced onion and garlic until transparent.
* Add the sliced mushrooms and fry over a high flame until the juices run and boil away.
* Add the wine and reduce until almost boiled away.
* Meanwhile ... in a large pot, bring the stock or water/stock cube to the boil.
* Add the kritharaki and bring back to the boil.
* Cover the pan and gently simmer until the pasta is cooked through (generally at least 20 minutes), adding more stock or water if necessary. Make sure the cooked pasta is still quite moist.
* In a warm bowl, combine the Kritharaki and the mushroom mixture and bring to the table.
* Serve with grated hard cheese.

Macaroni Verdi (makes you sing)

Ingredients for 4

350 g of short macaroni
60 g (half a cup) of pitted black olives
Finely grated hard cheese, e.g. Parmesan
450 g large ripe tomatoes
60 g of grated medium hard cheese, e.g. Cheddar or Kefalotiri
2 tbsp olive oil
Chopped or hand-torn fresh herbs of your choice

Method

* In a large pan boil a good litre of water, to which add a half-teaspoon of salt or 1 chicken stock cube. Add the macaroni and cook until tender (around 6-8 minutes).
* Skin the tomatoes (cut a cross in the bottom and immerse in boiling water for around a minute; the skins will then slip off). Cut in quarters and squeeze out and discard the seeds. Coarsely chop the flesh.
* Drain the macaroni and put in a shallow baking dish; add the tomatoes, olive oil and olives. Put in herbs (I recommend basil), sprinkle with black pepper and salt if needed and stir.
* Sprinkle medium-hard cheese on top and then the hard cheese and put the dish under a very hot grill until the top is brown.

Serve sizzling hot with a green salad and fresh bread.

Pancakes

Basic Pancake Mixture (for 8-12 pancakes)

100 g of plain or village flour
1 egg
30 cl milk
A pinch of salt
1 tbsp of sunflower oil, plus oil or butter for frying

Method
* Sift the flour and salt into a large bowl and make a hole in the middle.
* Mix in the egg and half the milk with a whisk.
* Beat briskly until well-mixed and bubbles start to appear on the surface.
* Add the remaining milk little by little, then the tbsp of sunflower oil, beating continuously.
* Cover the bowl and stand in a cool place for half an hour.
* To cook, heat the pan and put in a TINY knob of butter or a few drops of oil and swirl over the base.
* Take a small ladle, or two tbsp of the mixture and put into the pan, quickly shaking it to ensure it runs all over the base. Cook until brown and then turn over and cook the other side. The objective is to get a nice, thin, even pancake.
* Remove and repeat, remembering to stir the batter mixture regularly.

Savoury Pancake Fillings:

* Chopped cooked spinach or lahana, mixed with grated Kefalotiri or Tilsit. Roll the pancakes and cover with a Bechamel sauce and grated hard cheese and put in a very hot oven for 10-15 minutes.
* Chopped chicken fillet and mushrooms, fried in butter and tossed in a little double cream.
* Chopped bacon and onion fried with a crumbled sage leaf. Stuff the pancakes and place in a shallow dish. Surround with a home-made tomato sauce, top with grated cheese and brown under a hot grill.
* Defrosted North Atlantic frozen prawns, covered in a little Bechamel sauce.
* A Ragu (Bolognese sauce). Cover filled pancakes with Bechamel and grated cheese, put in hot oven for 10-15 minutes and, Presto, you have a close relative of Cannelloni.

English Yorkshire Pudding

Ingredients for a Pud for four

3 heaped tbsp plain flour
1 egg

1 cup of one part milk and three parts water)
Salt and ground black pepper

Method

* In your food processor whiz (or beat in a bowl if you like) flour, salt and pepper and egg.
* Dribble in milk and whiz/beat until you have a quite thin batter with bubbles on the top.
* Cover and set aside for 45 minutes.
* When ready to cook, beat again to form the bubbles and pour into roasting tray, under or round the meat. 45 minutes in fairly hot oven -- wizard!

French Yorkshire pudding

An odd one this - more like a choux pastry than Yorskshire pud., but tasty and fun nonetheless.

Ingredients

280 ml milk
4 tbsp softened butter
155 g self-raising flour
Dripping, lard or oil

Half tsp salt
4 eggs
Quarter tsp pepper

Method

* Put the milk into a small thick saucepan.
* Add butter and heat to boiling, making sure butter has melted.
* Trickle in the flour and let the milk seethe over it.
* Remove from the heat and beat/stir with a wooden spoon until absolutely smooth and thick.
* Add one egg, salt and pepper to the mixture and whisk until smooth, adding three more eggs, whisking as you go.
* In a 25cm round oven-proof dish, cover the base with melted dripping, fat or oil.
* Tip in the pudding mixture and use two forks to s-t-r-e-t-c-h it out roughly almost to the edge.
* Put on top shelf of oven heated to 225°C until as light as air and beautifully risen. Serve with roast meat, vegetables and English mustard.

Fish

Feuilleté de Saumon Fumé

Ingredients for 4-6 servings

225 g frozen puff pastry
225 g smoked salmon
1 can "Baxters" Lobster Bisque

2-3 King Prawns per person or a tbsp of shrimps
Thinly sliced cucumber

Method
* Defrost the pastry. Roll out just a little – you want nice fat chunks of puff psatry.
* Cut into four/six rectangular pieces, place on a baking tray, brush with beaten egg or milk and cook according to maker's instructions (About 20 minutes at 220°C)
* Warm, but do not boil, the Lobster Bisque, adding two teaspoons of brandy. De-frost prawns or shrimps and put into the warm oven for a few minutes.
* Peel and slice very thinly 1-2 small cucumbers.
* When you are ready to serve, on warmed plates, ladle out a covering of the Bisque. Swirl a little double cream into it.
* Cut each piece of pastry horizontally in half. Put a portion of smoked salmon on the bottom and put the top on. Place a piece in the centre of each plate.
* Lay the prawns or shrimps round and put the sliced cucumber around the edge of the plate. Garnish the pastry top with a small sprig of parsley.

Serve as a starter for six or main dish for four with broccoli and salad.

Good flavours like smoked salmon and lobster need a fairly robust and fruity dry or medium-dry white wine.

Omelette Arnold Bennett

Allegedly the invention of novelist and long-time London "Evening Standard" theatre critic, Arnold Bennett, in the 1920's, and to be found to this day on the menus of clubs and restaurants around Fleet Street. It is a splendidly rich and tasty concoction.

Ingredients for 3-4 portions
6 large eggs
250 g of smoked haddock fillet
1 small carton of double cream

125g grated cheddar, or similar, cheese
1 tbsp finely grated Parmesan cheese
Salt and black pepper

Method
* Poach the smoked haddock in milk in a shallow pan. When flaky, remove the skin and discard the milk, or give to the cat. Leave the flaked fish in the pan.
* Add the grated cheese and mix gently into the fish, over a medium heat. After a minute or two, remove from stove and set aside.
* Break six eggs into a large bowl and beat well. Add salt and black pepper and a pinch of Cayenne if you like.
* Turn on your grill to high.
* In a heavy, medium-sized frying pan, heat the oil and butter until sizzling. Add beaten eggs and cook over a medium heat. With a fork or spatula continually turn the egg mixture from the bottom of pan upwards and let the liquid egg run into the space.
* When the eggs are nearly set, but still juicy-looking, spread the warm mixture of smoked haddock and cheese on the top of the egg, pour the cream over evenly and finally sprinkle the Parmesan over the top.
* Put the pan under a hot grill (with the handle sticking outside, naturally!) and get the top brown and sizzly.
* Serve at once. Make sure everyone's in position to enjoy it just as soon as it comes to the table! If you've used a non-stick pan, you can slide the omelette onto a large warmed plate or serving dish—but remember, don't fold it!

Two-Flavoured Salmon in Cream

Ingredients, for one hearty or two modest portions

1 frozen Norwegian salmon fillet
1 can of Norway Gold slightly-smoked salmon fillet in oil
1 small cucumber, peeled and sliced
A good knob of butter
1-2 tbsp of cream (UHT is fine)
Salt and pepper
A little fresh dill, if you have it, chopped

Method
* Defrost the salmon fillet (this will take about an hour unless you use a microwave).
* In a non-stick frying pan or skillet melt the butter and gently sauté the salmon fillet until almost done.
* Open the can of slightly-smoked salmon, drain off most of the oil and gently put the salmon fillet into the pan.
* Dot the sliced cucumber around the fillet and sauté for a little while in the buttery juices.
* After a minute or two, add the cream and let it heat through. Sprinkle over some black pepper and a little salt (not much) and the dill, if you have it.

Serve with small, lightly boiled minted potatoes tossed in a tiny bit of butter (if you really are in a hurry, canned potatoes will do) and some frozen peas (unfrozen and cooked very lightly, of course).

Fish, Steamed with Fresh Ginger and Spring Onions.

Something a little different with a rather oriental flavour. The nicest fish I know cooked this way is sea bass, but any good cut of firm white fish will give you a delightful and not rich, main dish. For four servings you need about 150 grams of fish per person. It helps to have a steamer, but if you haven't, you can improvise by standing a suitable dish on top of a pan of simmering water and covering it.

Method

* Slice lengthways some blanched and peeled almonds, (about 60 g). You can also use almond flakes. Turn them in a tiny drop of oil in a hot frying pan until they are lightly browned. Set aside.
* Take the fish and lay inside your steamer top or on an oiled enamel or Pyrex dish. Spread the grated peeled ginger and sliced spring onions over the top. Sprinkle a little soy sauce and a dessert spoon of sunflower oil over and a few grindings of black pepper.
* Steam until the fish is cooked through, probably around 20 minutes.
* Transfer to a warm serving dish and sprinkle the toasted almonds over the top.
* Serve with stir fried vegetables into which you have tipped and mixed some thin noodles cooked in fish stock (a vegetable stock cube would do).

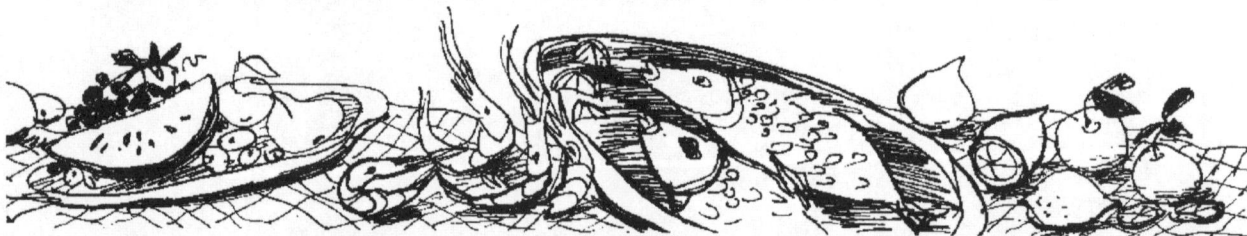

Basra Fish Pilaff

Something like this was once served to me by a charming Iraqi lady, Gita, who was no slouch in the kitchen, or at the table. It is not dissimilar from dishes served in southern Iraq, and I once had an earthenware pot sizzling with a good imitation in Kuwait, in the Hilton Hotel of all places.

Ingredients

450 g of firm fish fillet
1 medium onion, finely chopped
2 medium carrots, diced small
125 g fresh button mushrooms, sliced

1 clove garlic, chopped or crushed
1 tsp medium Madras curry paste
2 tbsp of olive oil or 15 g of butter
Cooked rice

Method

* Start by getting the rice on to cook. Wash 250 g of American or pilaff rice in a sieve. Into a medium saucepan put 1 l of light fish stock, or water with salt or a stock cube added (fish for preference, but chicken or vegetable will do). When the water/stock comes to the boil, add the rice, stir, bring back to the boil, cover and simmer for around 20 minutes or until the rice is of the texture you like.
* As soon as the rice is cooking, take a large skillet or frying pan and gently fry the fish in the oil or butter until it is just cooked through.
* Remove from the pan.
* In the remaining oil or butter (add a little more if necessary) fry the chopped onion, sliced carrot and crushed garlic until cooked through and lightly browned at the edges. Add the curry paste and cook on a low flame for a few minutes. Return the fish to the pan and, with a wooden spoon, carefully break it into pieces and stir

Continued on next page

Basra Fish Pilaff -- *continued*

round the vegetable and curry mixture. If the mixture is dry, dribble a little water over it and stir in. Cover the pan and simmer for a few minutes.

* Finally, carefully spoon the rice into the fish mixture and mix together. Heat all through. Serves 4 as a lunchtime or light dinner main course, or 6-8 as a starter.

Serving

I like this pilaff with salads: a dish of thinly sliced tomatoes dressed with oil and lemon and topped with chopped or hand-broken basil leaves, and another of sliced cucumber in yogurt and fresh mint. For those who like a more Indian flavour, add small dishes of sliced bananas; chopped raw onion mixed with vinegar and paprika; desiccated coconut and chutneys. Delicious! And to go with the light curry? A cool beer, perhaps; or a fairly gutsy rosé, Tavel for preference.

Lax Pudding

This recipe comes from Sweden and is fishy and comforting of a winter's day.

Ingredients (serves 4 as main dish)

200 g of Gravad-Lax
250 g of potatoes, peeled and sliced quite thinly
Several knobs of butter
3 tbsp of chopped fresh dill

Ground black pepper
4 eggs
40 cl of milk

Method

*   Butter a deep oven-proof baking dish.
*   Put the potatoes and salmon in layers.
*   Sprinkle dill and a little pepper between the layers. The first and last layer should be potatoes.
*   Beat the milk and eggs together and pour into the baking dish. Dot the top well with butter, grind some black pepper over it and bake in an oven heated to 175°C for about 1 hour.

The Swedes serve this dish with melted butter. I would regard this as optional! I would certainly have a green salad, some fresh bread and several glasses of a really crisp, fruity, dry white wine.

Fish Gateau (Serves 6 or part of a buffet)

Ingredients

175 g fresh white breadcrumbs
200 g tin of red salmon
120 g cream cheese
120 g of fromage fraiche or yogurt
4 salad onions, finely sliced

160 g melted butter
1 small tin of white crab meat
225 g of North Atlantic frozen prawns, defrosted
Juice of half a lemon
Salt and cayenne pepper

Method
* Put the breadcrumbs on a baking tray and put into a hot oven until crisp and golden. Remove and cool
* Drain the salmon and, in a mixing bowl, mash with a fork.
* Stir in the cream cheese, the fromage fraiche or yogurt, the finely sliced salad onions, half the crab and most of the prawns (keeping some for the garnish) and slightly less than a third of the melted butter, the lemon juice, salt and a pinch or two of cayenne pepper.
* Separately, mix the remaining butter with the breadcrumbs.
* Line a 18 cms (7 inch) cake tin with cling film.
* Put in the butter/breadcrumb mixture and press down firmly.
* Spread the fish mixture on the top and put in fridge for an hour or so to chill.
* Turn out, breadcrumb side upwards and garnish with crab, prawns, slices of cucumber, lump-fish roe, lemon slivers etc.

Red Mullet

A kilo of frozen red mullet fillets will go quite a long way - as far as six jolly good main course portions in fact.

De-frost them (3-4 hours in a warm room). Heat a large frying pan with an inch or so of light cooking oil. Roll each fillet in seasoned flour, dip in beaten egg and fry, skin side down for about three minutes. Turn over and cook top side until lightly browned. Turn skin-side down again and fry until skin is crisp. Serve with a tomato sauce, or home-made Sauce Tartare (Recipe on page 28) If you prefer, you may omit the beaten egg and simply fry the mullet fillets in seasoned flour.

You can use these fried fillets to make divine fish cakes. And don't knock them: fishcakes are "In" just now and rightly so. The parsley, onion and cumin in the following recipe combine with the red mullet to produce a rather splendid flavour.

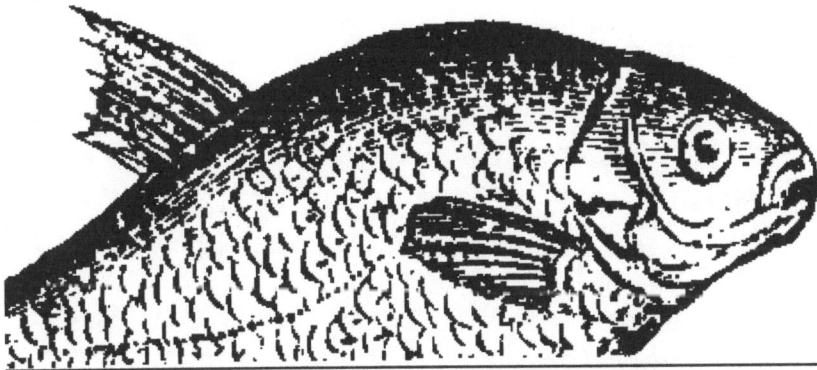

Red Mullet Fish Cakes

Ingredients for 6-8 servings

500 g of cold fried red mullets fillets
500 g of cooked mashed potatoes
2 good sized onions, finely chopped

2-3 good sprigs of parsley, finely chopped
1 level tsp powdered cumin
Salt and pepper

Method
* Crumble the cooked fish fillets into food processor and grind coarsely.
* Add the chopped onion and parsley and whiz for a seconds.
* In a large bowl, put the mashed potatoes, fish, onion and parsley. Add cumin, salt and pepper and, with a large spoon, mix together very well.
* Cover bowl and let it stand in fridge for one hour.
* Make flat round little patties from the mixture, around 6 cm across and 1.5 cm thick.
* Fry in shallow oil on a medium heat until brown on both sides.

You may coat the fishcakes with flour before frying, to make the outside a little crisper, or if you want the fishcake that has everything you may brush them with beaten egg, coat them with breadcrumbs and then fry them.
Serving suggestions: hot cooked beetroot, mashed with a knob of butter salt and pepper and chopped lightly cooked spinach.

WARNING Whatever you do, don't put the mashed potatoes into the food processor—you will get a gooey sludge that's extremely difficult to shape into fishcakes.

Red Mullet Fish Pie

For those who like fish pie, you can make a tasty version with the same ingredients I have given in the previous recipe. In a deep baking dish put a bottom layer of cooked mashed beetroot (about 500 g). Carefully lay on top the fishcake mixture. Top with grated Cheddar or Kefalotiri cheese and a sprinkling of Parmesan. Bake in a hot oven for around 20-25 minutes, or until the top is well browned.

Oriental Style Red Mullet

This little recipe is a rather jolly alternative to the fried stuff

Ingredients

500 g red mullet fillets
3 medium-large tomatoes, peeled and chopped
Half bottle dry white wine
1 tbsp olive oil

1 clove garlic peeled and chopped
Sprigs of parsley, thyme and fresh dill or fennel
1 pinch of saffron

Method
* Put mullet fillets in a solid frying pan and season with salt and black pepper
* Dribble the oil over and then cover the fish with the white wine
* Put in the tomatoes, garlic, herbs and saffon
* Bring to the boil and simmer until fish is tender

Petits Pots de Rouget (POTTED RED MULLET)

Ingredients

500 g defrosted red mullet fillets
1 large onion
125 g button mushrooms, sliced
225 g unsalted butter
1 cofsp ground mace or 2-3 pinches nutmeg

The juice of 1-2 lemons
2 good sprigs of parsley, finely chopped
Salt & pepper to taste
1 Des-sp dry sherry (optional)

Method

*   Finely slice and chop the onion and slice the mushrooms.
*   In your frying pan melt one quarter of the butter and fry the onion until it is transparent; add the mushrooms and cook for about five minutes, stirring from time to time. Remove from the pan and put in your food processor. In the same pan, melt some more butter and fry the red mullet fillets until they are cooked through, turning once. Remove and put in the food processor.
*   Now add the lemon juice, spices, the chopped parsley, the remaining butter and the dry sherry.
*   Whiz for about 30 seconds, until you have a nice, slightly rough-textured mixture. Taste, and season with salt and pepper.
*   Spoon the mixture into 8-10 small ramekins or into one good-sized shallow dish. Cover and refrigerate for at least four hours.

This dish is better if it is made the day before it is to be used and will keep for several days afterwards. It will also freeze. This may be served as a starter or as a main dish, in which case some prawns, phoney crab tails, scampi tails or—if you are in Rolls Royce country—plenty of king prawns may be added, with a fresh green salad.

Red Snapper Fillets with Multicoloured Peppers

Ingredients (for 6 people)

750 g of frozen red snapper fillets
1 red, 1 green and 1 yellow pepper
3 courgettes, each cut lengthways into 8 strips
2 medium onions, sliced into thin rings
8 tbsp olive oil

1 large or 2 medium cloves of garlic
2 pinches of dried tarragon or 1 sprig of fresh, chopped
1 large tomato, skinned, de-seeded and finely chopped
250 ml of medium-dry white wine

Method

*   Defrost the fish (it will take four/six hours depending on thickness).
*   Cut into pieces, allowing two for each person. Coat all the pieces with flour and set aside.
*   In a large frying pan, heat three tbsp of the oil and fry the onion until transparent.
*   Add the peppers and courgettes and fry for five/six minutes, stirring frequently. Remove from the pan and keep in a warm oven.
*   Add three more tbsp of the oil. Fry the fish pieces on a medium heat until lightly browned on both sides. Remove from the pan and put in the warm oven.
*   Add the last of the oil and stir-fry the chopped tomato for two minutes.
*   Add the wine and the stock and reduce about one-third by boiling for two to three minutes. Season to taste.
*   Put the fish on a serving dish, surround with the vegetables and pour the sauce over.
*   Decorate with a parsley sprig or two.

Serve with chunks of fresh bread and a green salad.

Seafood 'Walewska' (4-6 servings)

A super starter that never fails to please.

Ingredients

350 g filleted fish - cod, haddock, red snapper
250 g defrosted North Atlantic frozen prawns
125 g mushrooms, thinly sliced
Half litre of Bechamel or white sauce (Pages 39 – 40)
1 tbsp tablespoon dry sherry
60 g grated Parmesan cheese

Method

* Take a good knob of butter and melt in a small frying pan.
* Fry the lightly seasoned sliced mushrooms, turning from time to time until the juices have evaporated. Remove and set aside.
* Poach the fish fillet in milk and a little butter, salt and pepper. When just cooked through, remove from the pan and reserve the milk mixture (which should be used in the Bechamel sauce); skin the fish if necessary and flake coarsely.
* Mix together the cooked mushrooms, fish and prawns.
* Take one large or four/six small heatproof dishes and spoon in the fish mixture.
* Stir the dry sherry into the Bechamel sauce and pour over the fish.
* Sprinkle the grated Parmesan cheese over the top and put under a hot grill until top is nicely brown and bubbling.

Squid & Broad Beans

Ingredients for 6 servings

1 k of fresh or defrosted frozen squid, cleaned.
1 medium onion and 2-3 garlic cloves, finely chopped
1 k of small, tender broad beans (frozen ones are OK but should need very little cooking)
2 sprigs chopped parsley
2 tsp paprika
25 cl of water or fish stock
3 tbsp olive oil
1 small bay leaf
Salt and pepper

Method

* Heat the oil in a large, deep, heavy frying pan or saucepan and cook the onions and garlic until transparent
* Add parsley and fry for two minutes
* Stir in the paprika and add the squid
* Fry for five/six minutes, stirring regularly
* If using fresh ones, add beans and bay leaf and water or stock
* Season to taste
* Cook on low heat until squid is cooked through and liquid is reduced to an oily sauce. If you are using frozen beans add when squid is almost cooked through and cook until beans are tender.

Serve with a crisp green salad, or lightly cooked broccoli, and plenty of hot fresh bread.

Sweet & Sour Prawns

Ingredients for basic sweet and sour sauce

1 tbsp sunflower oil
1 cabbage leaf, very finely shredded
1 smallish carrot, very finely sliced, or grated
1 green pepper, de-seeded and finely sliced
2-3 salad onions, finely sliced
1-2 cloves of garlic, finely chopped or minced

3 tbsp wine vinegar
2 tbsp caster sugar
2 tsp tomato purée
1 tbsp of Soy Sauce
1 tsp grated fresh ginger, or ginger powder
Half tsp cornflour

Method
* Put the cornflour into a cup and mix in 6 cl of water.
* In a medium non-stick frying pan or work, heat the oil until it starts to smoke.
* Hurl the cabbage, carrot, green pepper, spring onions and garlic into the pan/wok and stir furiously in hot oil for a minute or two.
* Now stir in everything else except the cornflour mix. Make sure everything is well mixed together.
* Add the cornflour mix, with further water if you want the sauce a little thinner. Grind some black pepper over your sauce.

At this time you would add the sauce to the meat or fish of your choice, or put that in the wok with the sauce and bring it to the table.

Now for the Prawns. Defrost some cooked Atlantic prawns and just add to the sauce. Or, if you've recently won the lottery, defrost, shell and grill King Prawns and serve with (not in) your sweet and sour. My personal preference is to have plain boiled or steamed rice with sweet and sour dishes.

Beef

Beef and Veal

Local beef is something relatively new in Cyprus and for resident foreigners and visitors the appeal is the price as well as quality. Fillet is within most peoples' compass and it is very good. There is little dividing line between beef and veal – the latter simply being young beef and not the intensively reared white meat one finds in northern Europe. So the two are virtually interchangeable in recipes. Especially in hot weather large lumps of roasted meat are not the ideal home recipe – but, of course, they are to be found wherever there are ex-pats, in clubs, hotels and restaurants. There there are marvellous Sunday roasts and buffets which really make cooking a roast at home superfluous!

All the kebab and grill recipes in this book can use fillet or other grilling steak and most stewing steak is pretty tender, seldom needing more than an hour in the pot. I have chosen a small but varied selection of recipes, with a decidely international flavour.

Hungarian Steak Sandwich

Short order cooks love beef, because there are so many ways to grill or fry it (Season after cooking). Simple fine-ground beef patted into burgers and quickly fried makes a marvellous base for sauces, salads and vegetables. If your butcher will slice some beef fillet very thinly for you, (it *is* possible, of course, to do this yourself) you can try this **Hungarian steak sandwich.**

Ingredients, for six portions

12 thin slices of fillet steak
6 thin slices of pork fillet
6 slices streaky bacon, each cut into 4 strips

Mixed mustard
Salt and pepper

Method

* Season the steak slices with salt and pepper
* Spread one side of steak slices with mustard
* Make a sandwich, putting one slice of pork between two slices of steak (mustard side inwards)
* Slice bacon into long strips
* Make four slits in the "sandwich", one near each corner, and thread the bacon strips through to hold it together.
* Under a hot grill, or in a non-stick frying pan, cook the sandwiches on both sides until done all the way through.

You may serve these delights with chips and salad, or in a piece of hot "Pitta" bread, with olives, gherkins, pickles and salad on the side.

The classic beef stew of Cyprus is the **Greek Stifado,** made from beef, onions, tomatoes, red wine and fresh herbs. Similar dishes are to be found throughout European cookery. In Belgium, for example, they substitute their fine lager beer for the wine. It's a lovely dish and it's called **"Carbonade à la Flamande",** which can easily be adapted to Cyprus.

Carbonade à la Flamande

Ingredients for 4-6 portions
1 k lean stewing beef
500 g medium onions, peeled and sliced
2 tbsp olive oil or 50 grams rendered beef fat
60 cl KEO beer

1 tsp sugar
1-2 bay leaves and a pinch of thyme
Salt and pepper

Method

* Heat the oven to 170°C
* Cut the meat into 2.5cm square cubes and sprinkle with a little pepper.
* Heat the fat or oil in a deep oven-proof saucepan with lid and fry the onions until they are going golden. Remove from the pan and set aside.
* On quite a high heat, stir-fry the meat cubes until they are browned all over.
* Return the onions to the pan, stir and add sugar, salt, herbs and beer.
* Put the lid on the pan and cook in the oven for around two hours. Check and stir from time to time.

Depending on the cut of the meat you may need less or more time. Sometimes, if you are using a good frying steak, it will be cooked in a little more than an hour

NOTE: if you are using olive oil, then I suggest you omit the salt and add a beef stock cube to get a good beefy flavour.

This dish is a very tolerant one. It will stay in fine condition for some hours if kept warm and can also be re-heated, gently but thoroughly, very well.

Plain boiled, or jacket potatoes will "sup up" the delicious gravy perfectly. A green salad or quickly cooked crisp broccoli would complement the meat and tatties ideally.

Beef Stew with Fennel/Sicilian Beef

Ingredients
1 k lean tender stewing beef
1 large onion, 1 stick of celery, 1 clove garlic
1 small-medium head of fennel
2 tbsp olive oil

1 tbsp flour
450 g ripe tomatoes, skinned and chopped
15 cl Cyprus Muscat wine
Salt and pepper

Method
* Finely chop the onion, celery, garlic and fennel.
* Cut the beef into 5cm (2 inch) cubes.
* In a heavy deep pan, heat the oil and fry the chopped onion, celery and garlic until they are beginning to brown.
* Add the meat and stir round until the pink colour starts to brown, then add fennel.
* Sprinkle the flour, stir in and cook for a couple of minutes, stirring regularly.
* Add the Muscat and tomatoes, stir in, cover the pan and cook on a low heat for between 60 and 90 minutes, until the meat is tender. Add more liquid if necessary

Serve with boiled rice, noodles or boiled potatoes and a green salad with a lemony dressing.

Beef & Onions

Beef and Onions form the basis of some of the world's greatest and most popular dishes - carbonnade de boeuf, for example, or the much maligned hamburger. But the Chinese version has to be one of the best:

Ingredients

500 g of lean grilling steak
1 tbsp cornflour, salt and black pepper
4 medium onions or 10 salad onions
2 tbsp soy sauce and 2 of dry sherry

2 tbsp meat stock
2-3 pinches of sugar
2 tsp finely shredded ginger
3 tbsp sunflower oil

Method

* Slice the onions very thinly.
* Slice the beef into strips not more than 10 mm wide and 5 mm thick.
* Coat the beef strips in the cornflour, salt and pepper.
* Heat the oil until sizzling hot in a wok or frying pan.
* Stir-fry the beef and ginger for one/two minutes, turning constantly.
* Add the onions and stir-fry for not more than one minute.
* Add the sherry, soy sauce, sugar and stock and stir-fry for around half a minute. Serve with boiled rice.

I have not mentioned any of the more exotic Chinese sauces available in bottles. With a basic stir-fry you can have fun yourself, introducing Oyster Sauce, Black Bean Sauce, Yellow Bean Sauce, and so on. I always keep a bottle of Chili/Ginger sauce handy, which adds a dash to dishes like beef and onions.

Puff Pastry Steak

Easy to prepare. For 4-6 servings, you'll need...

225 g frozen puff pastry
450 g of fillet or rump steak
2-3 cups of tomato coulis (see page 35)

*   De-frost, roll out cut into 4-6 rectangles and cook the pastry on a hot oven (225°C)
*   Grill the steak to your preference. When cooked leave to stand for five minutes.
*   Slice the steak thinly and place between sliced pastry.

*   *Put on hot plates and surround with the tomato coulis.*

Filet de Boeuf en Croûte

Ingredients for 4-6 portions

1 k of fillet of beef
450 g of puff pastry
25 g of butter
1 egg yolk and a few drops of milk
Salt and pepper
Mushroom sauce (See page 32)
.

*   Make the mushroom sauce first.
*   If, as I have little doubt, you are using frozen puff pastry, defrost it. Next, pre-heat the oven to 225°C.
*   Remove any fat or sinew from the fillet.
*   Heat the butter in a large frying pan and brown the fillet all over, seasoning with salt and pepper.
*   Remove from the pan and put on a baking tray in the centre of the pre-heated oven, and bake for 10 minutes. Take out and let it cool completely.
*   Roll out the pastry in a shape to hold the fillet. Put the cooled meat in the centre and fold the pastry lengthwise. Using a little water, make a neat join along the top. Join the two ends in the same way.
*   Place on a lightly greased baking tray (join side down) and brush with the egg yolk-milk mixture.
*   Bake in a hot oven (225°C) for between 35-45 minutes. This should give you your fillet cooked *à point* (medium rare -- pink).

Serve with the mushroom sauce, broccoli florets and roast potatoes.

Steak Diane

Be warned - this is one of those 'sudden death' dishes that needs very speedy action with the frying pan, and it's not difficult to flame the kitchen as well as the steak if you're not careful!

Ingredients for 4 people

150 g butter
500 g fillet of beef
1 smallish onion, peeled and finely sliced
Juice of 1 lemon

1 des-sp Worcestershire Sauce
4 tbsp brandy
1 tsp sugar
Salt and pepper to taste

Method

* Cut the fillet into eight slices.
* Thwack each slice very thin with a heavy flat object.
* In a large frying pan, heat half the butter until it is beginning to turn brown.
* Fry the onion very quickly until the edges start to brown.
* Remove from the pan.
* Put the remaining butter in the pan and, when very hot, put in the fillet slices and brown very quickly on both sides. Remove from the pan.
* Put the onions back in the pan with the sugar, lemon juice and Worcester Sauce and swish about for a few seconds over high heat.
* Return the steaks to the pan, pour over the brandy and flame.
* Serve quickly from the pan to salivating guests.

Fondue Bourgignonne

A good party fondue is the Fondue Bourguignonne, but be prepared for very hot oil to sputter your tablecloth, your shirt or dress, your guests, the plates and everything else. Be careful of overheating the oil, which is far more dangerous than under-heating it. I recall the story of a friend's fondue party which produced such smoke that it filled the room and caused a guest with a weak heart to have a stroke -- so be warned!

Anyway, Fondue Bourguignonne is fun, even if you don't set the room on fire. You need a burner, a fondue pan if you have one, otherwise a deepish, heavy saucepan, preferably enamel. And, of course, skewers. The good thing about this is that you can mix and match all kinds of things: bits of beef fillet, pork, veal, chicken, fish, prawns, mushrooms, onion, green pepper and so on. In fact, I rather like to put two or three things at once on a skewer. You make up your selection, stick it in the bubbling oil and watch very carefully that your neighbour is not nicking your skewer. Then you take it out and you have a selection of dips. This can be curry-flavoured mayonnaise, a tomato coulis, a garlic sauce, a cream or cheese-based one, or a green one like guacamole. I think it's rather nice to serve this with things that you can easily spear with your skewer or a fork: small roast potatoes, mushrooms (unless these are on offer for the fondue), florets of cauliflower or broccoli, quartered tomatoes, chunks of cucumber and so on.

With this sort of fry up you are getting into tempura country -- the nice Japanese light batter into which seafood, lean chunks of meat and vegetables are dipped and then deep-fried. But this must wait for another time.

The Burgundians have a variation on boiling in oil -- BOEUF A LA FICELLE -- which has pieces of fillet of beef threaded with a string, which the diner plunges into boiling stock, and this is delicious.

Beef Fondue

Ingredients

1 l of beef stock, or a stock made from vegetables and beef stock cubes
4 100g fillet steaks, fat removed and cut into slices.

The method is simply to boil the stock and put in the meat for something under 10 minutes.

A sauce made from some more beef stock, some creamed horseradish, cream, mustard, salt and pepper, thickened with a little cornflour, is delicious with this. The French eat it with this sort of sauce and a variety of pickles and chutneys, of which pickled plum is well recommended. This is simply large plums, stones removed, some red wine, some wine vinegar, sugar, mixed spice, salt and pepper, boiled up and simmered for 10 minutes and served cold.

Sukiyaki

For this dish you need some Japanese ingredients, especially with the stock: seaweed, for example; fish sauce and soy sauce. But you may be able to find bottled Sukiyaki sauce. If you can't you would simply have to experiment.

Frankly, I would start with a stock made with some vegetables, a beef cube and some soy sauce. Anyway, you will need the following ingredients.

Ingredients

1kg of good, lean, tender beef
250gr plump noodles, cooked until al dente
If you can find it, 2 cakes of bean curd, which you have grilled
6 salad onions, cut into strips
12 small mushrooms (shitaki or similar if you can find them in the market)
A selection of tender vegetables, such as green beans, little bits of cauliflower, very thinly sliced carrot or pieces of cabbage
Several cups of the aforementioned stock

If you can find, or grow them, a few fresh bean sprouts wouldn't go amiss

Method

* Put the cooked noodles in a bowl, sprinkle with a little stock, cover and keep warm.
* Cut the beef into very, very thin slices and put half of it neatly onto a large plate. Cube the bean curd. Arrange half of the spring onions, mushrooms and your selection of vegetables on the platter.
* In your electric skillet, on-the-table pan or whatever, melt 60gr of Atora beef suet and then add one cup of stock.
* Then, very artistically, arrange the meat and vegetables in the bubbling stock and cook gently. The sauce at the bottom should be quite boiled down, but don't let it go dry, adding more stock from time to time.
* Put more ingredients in as necessary.

I like this served the Japanese way, with a beaten egg in a little bowl in front of you. With your chopsticks, you swirl around the meat or veggie pieces in the stock, dip it in the egg and presto -- absolutely delicious! The noodles accompany.

You can drink a light red wine with this if you like, but I can tell you that Japanese or Chinese rice wine (sake), slightly warm, in a little bowl, is lovely.

To conclude this section, why not consider a touch of luxury? This is a spelndid dinner party recipe which uses a good fizzy wine to give it sparkle..

Veal Kidneys in Champagne with Stuffed Peppers
Ingredients for six persons

2 veal kidneys
2 tbsps whisky
100 grams of unsalted butter
100 grams of button mushrooms, each cut into four slices
1 large salad onion, finely chopped
2 tbsps thick fresh cream
20 cl Champagne or other good sparkling wine
6 slices of white sandwich bread, crusts removed.
1 level cofsp of medium curry powder
Salt and pepper
Olive oil
Butter

For the stuffed peppers

6 small-medium sweet peppers
75 grams long-grain rice.
1 medium onion, peeled and finely chopped
25 grams unsalted butter
50 grams Cyprus sultanas
20 cl water or chicken stock
Olive oil
Salt and Pepper
Butter

Method.... first stuff your peppers
*   Heat oven to 230°C
*   Cut round the top of the sweet pepper to remove the core and the seeds from inside.
*   Blanch in boiling water for 4-5 minutes. Remove. Drench in cold water and set aside.

* In a good sturdy medium sized saucepan, heat a knob of butter until sizzling and fry the onion quite slowly until the edges begin to brown.
* Add the rice, stir to cover with the butter, then add the water/stock.
* Bring to boil, turn down heat, cover and cook slowly for about 20 minutes.
* While rice is cooking, put the sultanas in a bowl and pour over some boiling water and let soak until rice is cooked. Then mix them into it. Set aside.
* Now fill the de-topped peppers with rice mixture, brush them with olive oil and place them on an oiled baking tray.
* Put the tray of stuffed peppers into the middle of the oven and bake for about 20 minutes.

Meanwhile....cook your kidneys
* Probably there will be no fat on your kidneys, in which case brush them quite liberally with olive oil. Sprinkle them with salt and pepper.
* In a heavy pan (a two handled frying pan is best) bake the kidneys for 15-20 minutes, or until done to the degree of pinkness you want.
* Remove kidneys from the oven and pour the whisky over them. Over a burner, flame them. Remove kidneys and keep them warm.
* Heat the butter in the pan and gently sauté the salad onion and the sliced mushrooms.
* Add the champagne or sparkling wine and simmer bubblingly until it is reduced by half.
* Stir in cream and curry.   Bubble a little and reduce some more. Add a little butter and whisk to perfect the sauce. Season to taste.   Set aside keeping warm.
* In a sturdy frying pan, put some olive or sunflower oil and fry the squares of bread until crisply golden on both sides. Put them on a good-sized heated platter.
* Carve the kidneys into nice thin slices and arrange them on the fried bread.
* Finally pour the sauce over the kidneys and arrange the stuffed peppers between the kidney portions.

Ossobuco alla Milanese

Ossobuco a la Milanese has a lovely ring to it. It sounds very glamorous, but in fact it is braised shin of veal. It is my understanding that you can no longer buy such parts of the animal in Britain any more, but you can in Cyprus, where the "shin of veal" is shin of young beef and is therefore ideal for this particular dish. It is not difficult to make, and it is completed by *Gremolada*

Ingredients for 4 servings

4 pieces of shin of veal, each about 4cm (1½") thick
1 tbsp of flour
50g of butter
1 cup of Pasata, or 2 medium tomatoes, skinned, de-seeded and whizzed in your processor for a few seconds

6 cl (½ cup) of dry white wine
The grated rind of half a lemon
1 clove of garlic, peeled and finely chopped
1 sprig of parsley, finely chopped

Method

* Coat the meat with flour all over.
* In a large, heavy stew pan melt the butter and fry the meat, browning it on all sides.
* Slowly pour in the wine and simmer until it evaporates.
* Add the Pasata or tomatoes, put the lid on, and leave to simmer on a very low heat for about 1½ hours, stirring quite frequently.
* If necessary, add a little stock or water. However, the sauce should stay quite thick.
* The meat is done when it comes away from the bone. Remove the bones and prepare your *Gremolada*.
* Chop the parsley, the lemon rind and the garlic very finely and sprinkle over each piece of meat. Simmer for a few more minutes and serve very hot.

"*Next time you order Suckling Pig, I suggest you find out how big it is*"

Pork

Pork has that connotation of "not being as good as other meats" – perhaps because of its forbidden nature in the religions of Islam and Judaisim. Nevertheless, it is among the most consumed meats in the world and modern farming, butchery and refrigeration have given the lie to the old English adage: "Never eat pork when there's an 'R' in the month". In Cyprus, in my lifetime, it has replaced the former rather scrawny and tough sheep and goats as the staple meat. Because, it is said, pork doesn't freeze (I confess I never have any trouble doing so) it was not imported. Thus, with government help, it has become a major industy and pork is everywhere – in the barbecued dishes, ranging from whole pigs to tiny kebabs, and in a huge range of hams, sausages and cured meats of all kinds.

Butchers now cater for foreigners and you can get all the cuts you know and love, as well as joints ready for roasting with a skin that will produce excellent crackling (all you do is score, or pierce the skin all over and rub salt into it). Most of the chicken recipes in this book could use pork as a substitute. Here, then, are not typically Cypriot dishes, except *Afelia*, which I hearily commend, but a small cross-section of styles.

Pork & Peas
Ingredients for 4 servings

500 g lean loin or fillet of pork, cut into 2cm cubes
1 good-sized onion, peeled and sliced
1 tbsp flour
45 cl stock (use home-made if you can, or a pork or chicken stock cube in boiling water)
230 g peas (freshly shelled or frozen)
1½ tbsp olive oil
2-3 cloves
A couple of pinches of nutmeg
1 tsp of fresh oregano, or 2 tsp of dried
About a dozen black peppercorns

Method
* Heat oven to 180°C
* Toss the pork cubes in the flour, coating them well.
* Heat the oil in a medium flame-proof casserole and fry the pork until lightly browned all over. Add the sliced onion and carry on frying, stirring regularly.
* Turn the burner to low and, if there is any flour remaining, add to the pan and cook for a minute or two, stirring.
* Stir in the stock and cover the pan.
* In a mini food-mixer, or coffee grinder, whiz together the cloves, nutmeg, oregano and peppercorns until finely chopped and blended.

Continued on next page.

Pork & Peas - continued

*   Add to the pan. Salt and pepper to taste.
*   Put the pan in a pre-heated oven at 180°C for around 45 minutes. If you are using fresh peas, put these in after 15 minutes. If you have frozen, put these in after 30 minutes.
*   Have a look from time to time and give the pan a stir if necessary.

Serving

The sauce should be plentiful and tasty, so my serving suggestions would be something plain: boiled potatoes, plain boiled rice or noodles. For added colour, a dish of sliced, very lightly boiled carrots, tossed in a knob of butter, some black pepper and a little chopped parsley.

Peas & Ham

A QUICK SUPPER FOR FOUR......

Peel, slice and chop one onion. Fry in a knob of butter and two tablespoons oil until going golden. Add 300 g of frozen peas, stir and cover. Add a little water or stock as necessary, just enough to keep bottom from burning, put lid on pan and cook until peas are tender. Add 150 g of diced cooked ham or better still, Lounza. Mix over a medium heat and serve.

Afelia

Ingredients for 4-6 Servings

450 g of lean pork meat cut into small chunks
450 g of potatoes, peeled and cut into similar sized chunks
2 tsp of crushed coriander seeds (more if you like)
1 tsp of ground cinnamon
1 wine glass (20 cl) of fruity dry red wine
1 wine glass (20 cl) of good meat stock (or half a pork or chicken stock cube in boiling water)
Ground black pepper
20 cl of olive oil

Method

* Heat the oil in a large skillet (which has a lid) or shallow saucepan.
* Stir in the meat and brown quickly over a good heat (around five minutes).
* Add the diced potatoes and stir-fry for around five more minutes.
* Add coriander, pepper and cinnamon and stir well for a few seconds. Then tip in the wine and the stock and bring to the boil.
* Turn the heat down, put the lid on the pot and simmer for around 30 minutes, or until the meat is tender and the potatoes are cooked through but not falling apart. If your oven is hot the Afelia may be cooked there—I rather like the "casseroley" touch this imparts. Oven temperature:175°C
* Check the liquid level from time to time and top up with wine and/or stock if necessary. The sauce should be quite thick and rich.
* Serve as part of a Meze, or as a main course with crusty bread, a green salad and maybe a Bulgar Wheat (Pourgourri) pilaff.

The Spanish love to cook broad beans with their many sorts of ham, the famous *Serrano*, for instance. This roughly equates to a fairly mildly cured Cyprus Lounza, which works extremely well in this recipe.

Ham and Broad Bean Casserole

Ingredients for 4 as a main dish or 6 as a starter

1 large onion, chopped
2 good-sized garlic cloves, finely chopped
150 g of Lounza or gammon, cut into small cubes
750 g of fresh broad beans
2 medium-large ripe tomatoes, skinned and chopped
1 tbsp fresh breadcrumbs
10 cl of Keo FINO sherry or dry white wine

1 bay leaf
1 small sprig thyme finely chopped
2 sprigs parsley finely chopped
1 small sprig oregano finely chopped
25 cl of stock or water
4-5 tbsp olive oil

Method

* Heat the oil in a large thick casserole and fry the onions and garlic until transparent.
* Add the Lounza or gammon, the broad beans, bay leaf, the sherry/wine and stock/water, cover and simmer gently for about 30-40 minutes.
* Add salt and pepper to taste, the breadcrumbs and the finely chopped thyme, parsley and oregano. Stir well.
* Continue cooking until you have a thick, quite oily sauce.

Serve with a green salad and boiled potatoes, or "Garlic Pitta" [see receipe on P62.]

Note: if you use frozen broad beans, put them in after about 20 minutes of cooking.

Pork Fillet Vassos

Ingredients for 6-8 portions

3 pork fillets, each weighing about 300 g
350 g dried apricots
2 tbsp fresh or bottled green peppercorns

2 small cartons of whipping cream
2 wine glasses (40 cl) of dry white wine
2 tbsp Cyprus brandy
Salt and pepper

Method

* Wash and dry the apricots and cut in half.
* With a sharp knife make lengthwise incisions in the pork fillets, so as to make them spread out flat.
* Put the halved dried apricots in the middle of the fillets, sprinkle with salt and some of the green peppercorns and fold them lengthways.
* Melt a good knob of butter in an oven dish, put the stuffed pork fillets into it, and brush some of the butter over the top.
* Bake in a hot oven for around 30 minutes or until the pork is tenderly cooked through. Remove the fillets, and keep warm on a serving dish.
* Put the oven dish on the stove top, on a medium heat and stir the wine into the pork cooking juices. Add the brandy and cream, the remaining green peppercorns and a little salt. Cook gently for a minute or two.
* With a sharp carving knife, cut the stuffed pork fillets into slices and rearrange on the serving dish. Pour the cream/wine sauce around and top with a little chopped parsley.

Serve with boiled potatoes, rice or noodles and a green salad.

Sweet & Sour Pork

Ingredients: Basic sweet and sour sauce

1 tbsp sunflower oil
1 cabbage leaf, very finely shredded
1 smallish carrot, very finely sliced, or grated
1 green pepper, de-seeded and finely sliced
2-3 salad onions, finely sliced
1-2 cloves garlic, finely chopped or minced

3 tbsp wine vinegar
2 tbsp caster sugar
2 tsp tomato purée
1 tbsp of Soy Sauce
1 tsp grated fresh ginger, or ginger powder
Half a tsp cornflour

Method
* Put the cornflour into a cup and mix in half a cup of water.
* In a medium non-stick frying pan or wok, heat the oil until it starts to smoke.
* Hurl the cabbage, carrot, green pepper, spring onions and garlic into the pan/wok and stir furiously in hot oil for a minute or two.
* Now stir in everything else except the cornflour mix. Make sure everything is well mixed together.
* Add the cornflour mix, with further water if you want sauce a little thinner. Grind some black pepper over your sauce.

At this time you would add the sauce to the meat or fish of your choice, or put that in the wok with the sauce and bring it to the table.

The pork
Slice lean meat from leg, or pork fillet, into thin strips; coat with seasoned flour and quickly fry until golden-brown on both sides.

Cold Loin of Pork & Apple Sauce

Ingredients for 6-8 servings

1 filleted, cooked pork loin, weighing about 1-1.2 kilos
8 small or 4 large cooking apples or less-than-ripe eaters
1 wine glass of medium dry white wine
10 cl of mayonnaise
1 tbsp of *very* finely chopped fresh horseradish or ready-made horseradish sauce.
Salt and pepper to taste

Method

* "Earlier", cook your pork loin and let it cool.
* Peel, core and slice the apples thinly.
* Put the apples in a small stewpan with the glass of wine and cook on a medium heat. Remove, and in your food processor make into a purée.
* Return to the stewpan and, over a medium heat, let it thicken a little, stirring regularly.
* Let the purée cool, then add the mayonnaise, horseradish and seasoning. Mix well.
* Slice the pork loin into thin chops and arrange them on a large serving dish.
* Put the apple sauce in the middle and arrange a selection of pickles around (red cabbage, gherkins, onions, beetroot)

This is an accommodating dish that allows a dry white wine, a rosé or a light red.

Loin of Pork cooked in Milk

Not a combination to stir the desires immediately, but it should be remembered what a good effect milk has on liver, sweetening it and removing bitterness. In this dish the milk subtly enhances the pork.

Ingredients

1 k of boned pork loin
1 medium onion, peeled and chopped
1 medium carrot, peeled and chopped
2 cups warmed milk

2 garlic cloves, peeled and chopped
Salt and black pepper
1 sprig parsley, fine chopped
1 tbsp lard, rendered pork fat or oil

Method

*   In a large heavy oven proof pan, heat lard and brown the pork loin all over
*   Put in carrot and onion and cook until the onion is transparent
*   Add garlic and seasoning and then the warmed milk. Bring up to the boil
*   Cover, put down heat *very low* and simmer for about two hours
*   When the meat is cooked through, remove from the pot, put on a serving plate and keep warm
*   With a slotted spoon, remove the bits and pieces from the pan and whiz to a purée in your food processor
*   Return purée to the pot, stir with juice into a good sauce and pour this around the meat, finally, sprinkling some chopped parsley over the top.

Really fresh green vegetables, like crisp green broccoli, are called for here and something with which to sup up the juice, which I guarantee you will like, such as boiled potatoes or noodles.

A chilled Beaujolais would sit well with this main dish, a Fleurie, for example.

Lamb

Lamb is the meat of the Middle East, although in many countries goats are found in the same flocks, (probably to ensure the best quality of yogurt), especially in the Islamic world, where pork is either proscribed or barely tolerated for the infidel minority. I recall recoiling from my first contact with the tough meat from under-grassed, little-watered beasts, but all this has changed. If not in daily contact with green grazing, today's sheep have a good diet and plenty of water and produce a flavour not too far from that of Western European, New Zealand or Australian.

And lamb is delicious. For me there is nothing quite like a *gigot d' agneau*, the leg of lamb, with little garlic-filled slits in its skin, quite quickly roasted in a sprig or two of rosemary, French style, but not quite as *bleu* as the French like it, with a sauce made from red wine, chopped mint, a teaspoon of tomato purée and one of redcurrant jelly swirled in the meat juices as the joint nears readiness.

Lamb stews wonderfully and the two in the next pages will reward you and encourage you to vary the formula with various vegetables. People sing their praises of veal liver and kidneys, but I think that those of the lamb want a lot of beating. So a couple of ideas are to be found herein.

Shish Kebab

Ingredients for 6-8

1 k lean lamb meat, preferably from the leg
6 smallish onions, halved
2 large green peppers cut into 2.5cm squares
2-3 small tomatoes, quartered
Optional:
4-5 slices streaky bacon, cut into 2.5 cm strips and some small mushrooms

Method

*   Cube the lamb meat into 2.5 cm chunkets.
*   Count out all the pieces of your ingredients and divide them into eight.
*   Skewer each of the eight portions in an attractive order. Brush with barbecue sauce and put on a large tray.
*   Refrigerate for about one hour, turning from time to time so that each kebab skewer receives plenty of the barbecue sauce.
*   When you are ready, grill or barbecue quickly, sizzling the outsides and then carefully cooking through.
*   Serve with a rice pilaff or roast potatoes and Tabbouleh.

Barbecue sauce: recipe on page 31.

Shish kebab can be made with chicken, turkey, pork and beef fillet, or a mixture of these. For lovers of the "Surf and Turf" formula, contrast pieces of fillet steak with jumbo prawns.

Kofta

In Lebanon and neighbouring countries, a request for "Kebab" will bring forth this delicious minced charcoal grilled delight.

Ingredients (serves 4)

500-800 g lean lamb meat, preferably cut from the leg, amount according to appetites
1 fairly large onion, peeled and chopped
2 or 3 garlic cloves, peeled and chopped
A handful of parsley, chopped

Some sprigs of fresh mint, chopped
1 des-sp of powdered cinnamon (or vary to taste)
1 tsp of powdered cumin (or vary to taste)
Salt & pepper (according to taste)

Method

* Grind or mince the meat fairly fine. Put into a large bowl.
* Put the coarsely chopped onion, garlic cloves, parsley and mint into a food processor. Whiz until finely chopped.
* Remove and add to the meat.
* Sprinkle over the cinnamon and cumin and add the salt and black pepper.
* Mix well by hand or with a large wooden spoon.
* When thoroughly blended, cover the bowl and stand in the fridge for an hour or two.
* When the barbecue is ready, make sausage-shaped pieces from the meat mixture. You may skewer these, but I find it safer to use the double wire rack usually supplied with barbecues, lining up the Koftas, closing the rack and then grilling them quickly on both sides over very hot charcoal.
* Serve inside Arabic or Pitta bread with spicy salad and yogurt.

Country Style Casserole of Lamb

This is a Cyprus variation of an Italian lamb, potato and tomato dish.
Kid may also be used for this, and it's delicious.

Ingredients (to serve 6-8)

1 k of boned lamb or kid, chopped into good chunks
2-3 large onions, sliced
500 g of new or small potatoes, scraped or peeled
450 g ripe tomatoes, peeled, de-seeded and chopped
A sprig of oregano and a sprig of rosemary, finely chopped
25 cl of dry white wine
125 g grated Anari or Halloumi cheese
25 cl of olive oil
Salt and freshly ground black pepper.

Method

* Heat oven to 175°C
* Heat the oil in a large flame-proof casserole and fry the onion until soft and beginning to brown.
* Add the meat chunks and the herbs and cook on a high heat.
* Stir regularly until the meat is browned on all sides.
* Add the tomatoes and potatoes and the salt and pepper, mixing all the ingredients together.
* Sprinkle the grated cheese over the top, put the lid on the pan and cook in the oven at around 175°C for about 60 minutes or until the meat is tender.

Lamb Stew with Plum Jam

Ingredients for 4 servings

1 k of lean leg of lamb, taken off the bone
Seasoned flour
30 g of butter
1 tbsp of olive oil
2 medium-sized onions, peeled and sliced
6 medium-sized carrots, sliced
2 large potatoes, peeled and cubed

4 sticks of celery, sliced
2 sharp apples, peeled and sliced
Salt and freshly ground black pepper
50 cl of light stock (e.g. boiling water and one lamb or chicken stock cube)
2 tbsp of plum jam

Method

* Cube the lamb and roll in seasoned flour.
* In a large, heavy casserole heat the oil and melt the butter in it.
* Put in the lamb cubes, a few at a time, and brown them on all sides quickly, removing them as they brown, then set aside.
* Put in the onions, carrots, celery and apple and stir-fry until they are lightly browned, seasoning them with salt and pepper.
* Stir in a half-tbsp of the seasoned flour, then add the stock and stir well.
* Put the meat back in the pan, bring it to the boil, reduce the heat, cover and simmer for about one hour or until the lamb is tender.
* Finally, stir in the plum jam and taste for seasoning.

Kidneys à la Kensington

Ingredients for 4 servings

8 lambs' kidneys
2 medium-large onions, thinly sliced
1-2 cloves of garlic
200 g of mushrooms
1 des-sp of Worcestershire Sauce
1 des-sp of mixed English mustard

1 des-sp of tomato purée
10 cl of dry sherry
Chili pepper, or Tabasco sauce, to taste
50 cl chicken stock
Small sprig of thyme and 1 bay leaf, salt and pepper
A walnut-sized knob of butter and 2 tbsp of olive oil

Method

* Remove the suet surrounding the kidneys, take off the "skin" covering the kidney and cut away the gristly bit in the middle. Slice each kidney into around six/eight pieces.
* Heat the butter in a large, deep frying pan.
* When the butter is sizzling, turn down the heat and "sweat" the onions for 15-20 minutes, until the edges are beginning to brown and caramelise (this will produce a slight sweetness).
* Add the oil, turn up the heat and put in the garlic and mushrooms. Stir-fry on a high heat for around five minutes, until the mushrooms have cooked through.
* Turn the heat down a little and add the sliced kidneys. Cook the mixture for a further 10 minutes, stirring regularly.
* Now add the Worcestershire Sauce, mustard, tomato purée, red pepper or pepper sauce, sprig of thyme and bay leaf, and stir round for a minute or two.
* Pour in the stock, stir, cover the pan and cook gently on a low heat for 10 minutes.
* Serve with plain boiled rice, a green vegetable or a salad.

Liver & Onions with White Wine

Ingredients for 6 servings

1 k lambs' liver, thinly sliced

450 g onions, peeled and thinly sliced
2 wine glasses dry white wine
2 tbsp olive oil and a good knob of butter
Salt, pepper and a good sprig of parley, chopped

Method

*   Heat the oil and butter in a large sturdy frying pan.
*   Fry the sliced onions until golden.
*   Remove the onions from pan, leaving as much of the oil/butter as possible.
*   On quite a high heat, seal both sides of the liver quickly and then fry for a few minutes, turning once or twice.
*   When almost cooked to your taste (I like it pinkish inside) return the onions to the pan, add the wine, salt and pepper and simmer for a few minutes.
*   Sprinkle over the chopped parsley and serve.

TIP: Soak the sliced liver in milk for an hour or two before cooking - it will draw out any bitterness in the flavour

Chicken,
Turkey
and
Rabbit

Chicken, Turkey & Rabbit

In Praise of the Chicken

For the while, we who live in Cyprus don't have to worry about "Corn Fed", "Free Range" and such nomenclature. You can usually find good tasty birds, whole or dismembered (and sold, as 'parts' for a lot more money than the whole). Chicken features widely on our menus.

The chicken fillet is a wonderful invention although I don't suppose the chicken is very keen on being parted from it. I always have some in my freezer, which can be defrosted in five minutes in the microwave and set to good use to feed sudden visitors. Cubed and skewered with bits of bacon, mushroom, tomato and pepper and so on, chicken fillet makes splendid kebabs and, as the weather gets hotter, it can form the basis of delightful salads and other dishes.

Pasta freaks will enjoy spaghetti with a tomato sauce (see page 35) and a chicken escalope coated in breadcrumbs and fried. Here's how.

Chicken Escalopes in Breadcrumbs with Pasta & Tomato Sauce

*   Lightly toast or bake one Pitta bread.
*   In your food processor put broken pieces of the Pitta and make breadcrumbs.
*   In a shallow dish put the breadcrumbs and mix them with salt, pepper and a tablespoon of grated Parmesan cheese. Mix well.
*   Beat four chicken escalopes flat and dip them in flour.
*   Next, dip the floured escalopes into well beaten egg and make sure they are covered all over.
*   Take the egged escalopes and roll them in the seasoned breadcrumbs, making sure they are covered all over.
*   Gently fry until golden and cooked through. Serve.

Little Escalopes of Chicken, Muscat and Walnuts

Ingredients (for 4 servings)

3 tbsp of olive or sunflower oil
450 g of chicken fillet
50 g of flour, seasoned with salt and pepper
1 wine glass (20 cl) of Cyprus Muscat wine
1 wine glass (20 cl) of chicken stock

1-2 squeezes of lemon juice
40 g of butter
100 g of walnuts
Salt and pepper to taste

Method

*   With a sharp knife cut the chicken fillet into slices 6mm thick and beat them very thin; one good smack with a heavy flat object should suffice (I use a meat cleaver bought in a Chinese supermarket, but anything similar will do).
*   Dip the slices of chicken into the seasoned flour and make sure they are well coated.
*   Heat the oil in a frying pan on a high heat and when it is hot pop the chicken slices into it. Fry briefly for a minute or two until golden brown on both sides.
*   Remove meat from the pan and put on a warm plate.
*   Add wine, stock and butter to the pan and boil, stirring well, over a medium heat until sauce is reduced. Add a little lemon juice to give a slight sour-sweet flavour.
*   Put the meat back in the pan, add the walnuts and, after half a minute or so, serve.

A variation on this dish is to use mushrooms instead of walnuts. In this case, thinly slice and fry 6-8 mushrooms in a little butter before frying the chicken slices. When lightly browned on both sides, remove from pan and set aside. Then carry on as described above. It is also very good substituting the walnuts with slivers of toasted almonds.

Chicken Fillets in a Vermouth, Cream and Leek Sauce

Ingredients (4 good servings)

2 medium-sized leeks, chopped into rings
1 small pot of fresh or carton of long-life cream
Salt and pepper

4 boned chicken fillets
3 tbsp of Dry Cyprus Vermouth

Method

*   .   Put the chopped leeks (or large salad onions if leeks are not available) into a saucepan and cover with chicken stock or hot water to which a stock cube has been added. Bring gently to the boil and simmer until cooked through. Set aside.

*   In a medium-sized frying pan or skillet sauté the chicken fillets in a little butter until lightly browned on each side and cooked through.

*   Add the cooked leeks in their remaining liquid and the Dry Cyprus Vermouth to the chicken and simmer for three/four minutes. Add the cream and stir in. NOTE: if you find cream too rich you may add some more stock, or milk, which you may wish to thicken slightly with corn-flour (corn-starch). Make sure cream does not boil.

*   Season to taste, gently stir and serve.

As accompaniments I suggest plain boiled rice, noodles or boiled potatoes and broccoli if there is any around. If you want a second side dish, sliced mushrooms fried in a little butter. It's an accommodating dish for wine: a dry white, a rosé or a light red would suit! For a variation it may also be cooked using fish—some of the very meaty imported red snapper fillets to be found in many supermarket freezers are ideal, just poached in a little milk and butter, with the skins removed after cooking.

This is an excellent family or dinner party dish that is quick and easy to make. It can be partially prepared before the meal, then assembled and put in the oven for 15-20 minutes when *you are ready*.

Chicken and Lahana (Swiss Chard)

Ingredients (For 4-6 servings)

Meat from one medium-sized boiled chicken or 3-4 cooked chicken breasts
2 bunches of lahana (Swiss Chard)

About 1 l of Bechamel sauce (recipe, page 40)
125 g of Cheddar, Tilsit or similar cheese grated
1 tbsp finely grated Parmesan
Salt and pepper

Method

* Gently simmer the whole chicken in a litre or more of water, in which you have chopped an onion, 1-2 sticks celery, 1-2 carrots and a rasher or two of bacon. Add fresh herbs of your choice. When tender (about an hour) remove from the pot and take the meat from the carcass. Return the skin and bones to the pot and simmer a further hour or so to produce a good stock.
* Remove the choggiest parts of the stalks from the lahana, wash and chop coarsely. Cook for four/five minutes in a little boiling water. Remove and drain thoroughly.
* Make your Bechamel sauce.
* In an oven baking dish, place the cooked chicken and lahana, mix, and pour over the Bechamel sauce.
* Sprinkle the grated cheese over the top and put into a hot oven, near the top for around 15 minutes, until top is golden brown.

Continued on next page.

Chicken and Lahana- continued

If you are using chicken breasts:

* Cut the chicken into smallish cubes.
* Fry in plenty of butter (about 100 g)
* When the chicken is cooked thoroughly, sprinkle 2-3 tbsp flour over and mix in well. Keep turning for several minutes.
* Slowly add up to a litre of milk or milk and stock, stirring all the time to make your sauce. This does require care to avoid lumps. Add salt and pepper to taste.
* When you have got the consistency you want, add the mixture to the lahana in the oven baking pan, top with the cheese and put into the oven.

If you are not a meat eater, large sautéed or grilled mushrooms may replace the chicken.

Chicken Patrikios

This is another of those recipes you can make easily and quickly from things already in your freezer/fridge/cupboard. It is delicious and makes a simple dinner party main course, which can mostly be prepared in advance.

Ingredients for 4-6 servings

1 large onion, chopped
1-2 cloves of garlic, finely chopped (optional)
4 chicken fillets, cut into nuggets
2 tbsp flour

1 can of Cyprus artichoke hearts
450 g frozen peas
1 tub of sour cream
250 ml of chicken stock
Good knob of butter and 2 tbsp sunflower oil

Continued on next page.

Chicken Patrikios – *continued*

Method

* Roll the chicken nuggets in the flour, coating them well.
* In a large, deep frying pan with lid, heat the oil/butter and fry the onion (and the garlic if you want this extra flavour) until transparent.
* Add the chicken to the pan and fry on medium heat until light brown, turning regularly.
* Add the chicken stock and stir well. Lower the heat, put the lid on and simmer for about 10 minutes.
* While the pan is simmering, drain the artichokes and cut each one into 4-6 pieces. Put them and the peas into the pan and continue simmering. Don't let all the stock boil dry—add more (or a little water) if necessary.
* After about 10 minutes the peas should be cooked and you are ready to serve—all that remains is to stir in the sour cream, season to taste and put back on the heat for a minute or so.

If you prepare this dish in advance, do everything except adding the sour cream. When you are ready, re-heat the pan, put in the sour cream and proceed.

Serve with a finely chopped salad of cabbage, a lahana leaf or two, green and red pepper and cucumber, with a light oil and lemon dressing. Have potatoes if you will, or griddled Pitta Bread (brush a little oil on each side of the Pitta and either put under a hot grill for a minute or two or "dry fry" in a non-stick pan or iron griddle).

Steamed Chicken & Mushrooms

Ingredients

500 g of boned fresh chicken
3-4 medium sized flat mushrooms
2 slices of peeled ginger, chopped
1 tbsp dry sherry
1 tsp sugar
1 tsp cornflour

1 tsp sunflower oil
1 tsp salt
Freshly ground black pepper and pinch or two of red pepper

Method

* Cut the chicken into small pieces.
* Mix the chicken with the sherry, sugar, cornflour and salt.
* Slice the mushrooms and ginger very, very finely.
* Grease an enamel or Pyrex plate with a little oil, and place the chicken pieces on it.
* Put the mushrooms and ginger on top, sprinkle over the pepper and the sunflower oil.
* Steam vigorously for 20 minutes. Serve at once. (NOTE: if you don't have a steamer, stand the plate on a bowl in a very large pan one third filled with water, so that it is well above the water level—and keep the water bubbling reasonably)

Chicken with Almonds

Ingredients

1 small-medium chicken cut into 12 pieces
1 medium onion, finely chopped
3 sprigs parsley, chopped
1 good slice of village bread, crumbled
2 cloves garlic, finely chopped
Half coffee cup of blanched, peeled and ground almonds
1 tsp cinnamon

1 tsp turmeric
2-3 cloves, ground or finely crushed
5 cl lemon juice
10 cl Keo FINO sherry
Salt and pepper
4 tbsp olive oil for frying
Water or chicken stock as necessary

Method

* Take 2 tbsp olive oil, heat in a good heavy frying pan and turn the chicken pieces until the outsides are brown.
* Add the onion and cook until the edges are browning.
* Toss in parsley and turn.
* Remove from the pan and set aside.
* Put in the remaining two tbsp oil, heat and fry the bread and garlic.
* When nicely browning, remove and turn into your food processor. Whiz.
* Add all the other ingredients (except the chicken and onions!) and whiz again, until you have a nice stiff creamy mixture.
* Return everything to the frying pan, cover and simmer on a very low heat for a few minutes. If the sauce thickens too much add some stock or water.

Poule au Pôt

This is a classic French country dish, requiring of a large boiling fowl, really. But you can find pretty big birds in the supermarkets (and not just at Ayia Napa either) which, nevertheless, don't take much more than an hour to cook.

You need a good stuffing and a good vegetable stock, both of which I propose to you.

Ingredients for the stuffing:

100 g smoked ham or lounza, chopped
100 g breadcrumbs, either from fresh bread or dry ones which you have dampened
2 eggs
100 g chicken livers, fried in butter, cooled and chopped
25 g salad onions, chopped
2 cloves of garlic, peeled and finely chopped
Salt and pepper
A herb flavouring of your choice. I would suggest a little finely chopped thyme and sage and perhaps a sprinkling of cinnamon

For the **stock** you basically need 5 litres of liquid, for which you would need 3-4 vegetable stock cubes or the following:

4 large carrots
3 large onions
3 medium-sized leeks
2 stalks of celery

Continued on next page.

Ingredients for the Stock -- *continued*

A sprinkling of miscellaneous herbs or a bouquet garni
Black pepper
6 garlic cloves, peeled
Some veal bones

Method

* Prepare the stuffing: in a large bowl, mix together all the ingredients and season.
* Stuff this into the chicken, then sew up the neck, body and other orifices with a needle and thick thread.
* In a very large pot put the chicken and the 5 litres of water and bring to the boil.
* Simmer for about 10 minutes, taking the scum off as it forms.
* Add the bones, vegetables, herbs etc. (or vegetable stock cubes)
* On a low heat, simmer until the chicken is very tender and the legs will come away from the body. It should then be done.

You should be left with a stock that is delicious and, with very few additions and amendments, can make a fine soup with which to start the meal. Alternatively, there is plenty of liquid for a gravy, which can be supped up with fresh French bread or jacket potatoes. I think Poule au Pôt asks for a green salad to go with it. And something chilled and crisp to drink with it. A Sauvignon Blanc from Provence, perhaps, or a Californian Fumé Blanc, whilst in Cyprus, Salera white, Vasilikon, or the charming Semillon-Xynisteri blend from Fikardos, Ayia Irini.

Sweet and Sour Chicken

Ingredients

2 chicken fillets, cut into 2 cm nuggets
110 g peeled fresh, or canned pineapple, in chunks
1 large carrot, thinly sliced
1 green pepper, de-seeded and diced
3 salad onions, sliced
1 tbsp sugar
3 tbsp rice vinegar

4 tbs water
1 tbsp tomato ketchup
2 tbsp light soy sauce
1 tsp cornflour
3 tbsp groundnut oil and 2 tbsp water
2 cloves of garlic, peeled and sliced
2 tbsp rice wine or dry sherry

Method

*   Mix sugar in vinegar until dissolved and add ketchup and soy sauce. Mix well. Set aside.
*   Mix cornflour in a little water until smooth Set aside.
*   Heat heavy non-stick frying pan or wok and add oil.
*   When beginning to smoke, add chicken nuggets and briskly stir-fry for one minute.
*   Add garlic and stir fry for another minute. Then pour in wine or sherry and add the pineapple.
*   Now put in the other vegetables, except salad onion and continue stir-frying.
*   Pour in the vinegar/ketchup/soy sauce mixture, stir-fry for half a minute.
*   Add cornflour mix (well stirred) stir until sauce thickens, adding a little more water if necessary.
*   Serve at once topped with the raw, sliced salad onions, plus steamed plain rice, and chinese vegetables or an oriental salad.

Stuffed Boned Chicken

Open out a boned chicken, skin-side down. Make your stuffing from: 450 g of slightly fatty pork pieces, finely minced; 4 slices of streaky bacon, finely minced; 1 large onion and 6 medium-large mushrooms very finely chopped; 2-3 sage leaves, finely chopped and 1 flat tsp each of powdered cinnamon, cumin and garlic; a little salt and a generous sprinkling of freshly ground black pepper. Mix everything together in a bowl and then lay in a long sausage shape in the centre of the spread-out chicken.

Fold the sides and ends of the chicken over and either tie or, as I do, put some wooden kebab skewers through at strategic points, to prevent the poor stuffed boneless bird coming apart. Turn the whole thing skin-side up, brush a little oil over and roast in the middle of a hottish oven (200°C). This will take about an hour and a half. Turn once during cooking.

During the cooking a lot of lovely juices will be released. Drain them and put them in a small saucepan with a cup or two of water, a tablespoon of tomato purée (ketchup does as well, or better), a tablespoon of dry sherry and seasoning. Bring to the boil and thicken with cornflour (mix one heaped teaspoon in a cup with water and tip into the saucepan, stirring briskly).

Bring the masterpiece to the table and carve lovely succulent slices off. Add some sauce and serve with roast potatoes and a green vegetable. If there's any left (as if there will be!) it's super cold. Slices thinly and beautifully.

Spicy Stuffing

The classic Christmas stuffing, I suppose, is sausage meat and chestnut. But I prefer a spicier variety, which adds to the sausage meat an equal weight of finely chopped or grated carrot, onion, garlic and mushrooms, flavoured with cinnamon, cumin and turmeric. Traditionalists may drop the 'oriental' spices and substitute sage and thyme!

Ingredients:
Breadcrumbs, dried apricots chopped, sliced onions, sultanas, flaked toasted almonds, a spoon of tomato purée, seasoned and herbed to your choice, bound together with a beaten egg and a spot of brandy.

Sage & Onion Stuffing

Fresh sage and onion are the classic ingredients of stuffing for rich meats, such as pork and duck, but I love it in chicken and turkey, too.

Ingredients: 450 grams of onions, peeled and finely chopped; 100 g of *home-made* breadcrumbs, 6 fresh sage leaves, finely chopped; 25 g butter or 1 tbsp olive oil and salt and pepper.

Method: Put the chopped onion in a small pan and barely cover with water. Simmer for 10 minutes. Remove onions to a mixing bowl, keeping the water. Mix all other ingredients in and moisten with a little of the onion water until you have a well-bound mixture.   Then stuff your bird.

Moist breadcrumbs can be the vehicle for all kinds of variations of herbs and spices: thyme, oregano, garlic, parsley, and so on. Cold stuffing is delicious sliced and served cold or fried to a golden crispiness.

Turkey Triple

Ingredients for 4 servings

4 thick slices of turkey breast, beaten flat
8-12 very thin slices of Hiromeri
Thin slices of Kefalotiri, Cheddar or similar cheese
A few sage leaves
Seasoning to taste

Method

* In a large heavy frying pan or skillet melt a little unsalted butter and crumble in one or two sage leaves. Gently fry the turkey fillets until cooked through and lightly browned on both sides.
* In the pan, drape over each fillet the thin slices of Hiromeri (or very thin sliced lounza or ham if you prefer) and then the thin slices of cheese.
* Continue cooking on low heat until the cheese softens and begins to melt. Sprinkle some black pepper over the top and serve.

A sauce made from slightly thickened stock, a little tomato purée and a drop of white wine could "lubricate" this dish, or a straightforward home-made tomato sauce. Serve with pasta or minted boiled potatoes and a green vegetable.

Filleted Saddle of Rabbit

To serve four people you will need at least two rabbits, which you should cut into pieces—the back and front legs/chest and the saddle. Freeze all pieces except the saddle and the liver, for use in another recipe. With a very sharp, pointed knife carefully remove the two saddles of meat each side of the backbone and gently beat flat.

Ingredients for 4 servings

The filleted saddles from two rabbits
The rabbit liver, sliced into 4-6 slivers
1 large apple, cored, peeled and cut into 8 slices
1 egg
Several good knobs of butter

25 cl or more of dry red wine
1 tbsp tomato purée
1-2 sage leaves finely chopped
Salt and pepper

Method

* Dip the apple slices into flour. When well covered, dip into beaten, seasoned egg and fry in hot butter until golden on both sides. Set aside on a serving dish in a warm oven.
* Heat another good knob of butter in your frying pan and fry the rabbit saddles on a medium heat until golden brown on both sides and cooked through. When you turn them, add the sliced rabbit liver and cook on both sides. When all is done, remove from pan and put on the serving dish.
* De-glaze the pan with the red wine and reduce by one third. Stir in the tomato purée, salt and pepper. Add more red wine if necessary.
* Arrange the four pieces of saddle around the serving dish, with a slice of the fried apple on each side, each of which has a sliver or two of liver on top.
* Pour the wine sauce around the rabbit and apple and serve.

Rabbit Stifado

Ingredients (serves 4-6)

1 rabbit, about 1.5 k cut into 8-10 pieces
500 g small onions, peeled but not chopped
500 g ripe tomatoes, peeled and chopped
4 tbsp olive oil
2 bay leaves and pinches of fresh rosemary and oregano

25 cl meat or chicken stock
2 tbsp wine vinegar
1 des-sp sugar, salt and pepper
Up to 75 cl red wine
2 tbsp flour

Method

* Heat the oven to 175°C
* In a large frying pan, heat oil. Roll rabbit pieces in flour and fry in hot oil until browned all over.
* Add the onions and fry for around five minutes. You can use frozen baby onions, in which case de-frost them and proceed.
* Add tomatoes and cook for a further five minutes. Remove and put into a large oven-proof saucepan or casserole.
* De-glaze the pan with stock. With the wine, pour into the casserole.
* Put the lid on the pot and cook for three/four hours on a very slow heat or in the oven set at 175°C.

Serve with jacket or boiled potatoes, noodles or very fresh crusty bread, village salad and a robust red wine with good acidity.

Chicken Fillet Salad

Ingredients for 6 servings

1 450 g pack of tricolore pasta
6 chicken fillets (4 if they are large ones)
2-3 peeled, sliced cucumbers
3-4 spring onions finely chopped
1 cup of cooked peas

1 small can of sweet red peppers, drained and thinly sliced
Some green leaves, very finely sliced (cabbage, lettuce or lahana)
French dressing (see page 164)

Method

*   In a large pan boil a generous amount of water into which you have put a chicken stock cube or two.
*   Boil the pasta until *al dente* (still with a bit of bite in it). Drain and set aside in a colander to cool as quickly as possible.
*   While you are doing this, gently sauté the chicken breasts in butter and/or oil until cooked through. Set aside to cool.
*   In a large dish combine all the other ingredients except the vinaigrette. When the pasta and chicken are cool combine with the salady bits.
*   Sprinkle over the vinaigrette, top with some chopped mint or parsley and serve.

Accompany with fresh bread, some yogurt, and a tomato salad over which you have sprinkled some broken leaves of fresh basil and chives.

Pick a Pitta Pocket *or two* -- Cold Chicken Curry...*and more...*

Ingredients (for 2 large Pittas)

1 cooked chicken breast or similar weight of any
chicken meat
4 lettuce leaves

8 dried apricots, chopped
4 des-sp of mayonnaise
1-2 tsp of mild curry paste

Method

*   Thoroughly mix the mayonnaise and curry paste in a bowl.
*   Chop the cooked chicken meat and add it and the chopped apricots to the curry-mayonnaise, gently mixing together.
*   Slit open the Pitta bread pieces and line with the lettuce leaves.
*   Put equal measures of the chicken curry mixture between the lettuce leaves of each piece of Pitta and serve with a salad of freshly sliced tomatoes with basil.

You can also make your own favourites, but here are a few tried and trusted suggestions.

*   Coat the chicken breast with tandoori flavouring, grill brown on both sides, chop into pieces and slip into the lettuce leaves lining the Pitta; then spoon in some yogurt and chopped mint.
*   Streaky bacon, fried or grilled crisp, chopped and added to a finely chopped mixed salad of your choice. Put this in the Pitta and sprinkle with a few drops of chili sauce.
*   In a non-stick frying pan, with no oil or fat, fry slices of ham or lounza and some slices of halloumi cheese. When done, put into hot Pitta with slices of tomato or splashes of ketchup.

* Hard-boil an egg per person, cool in cold water, remove the shell and chop with 2 tsp of mayonnaise and a small onion, spring onions or chives. Put in Pitta with sliced cucumber and tomato.
* If you have a griddle or a toasted-sandwich maker, slice some Kefalotiri, Tilsit or Cheddar cheese and some ham or lounza, fill the Pitta and toast/griddle until the cheese is melted. A sort of "Cyprus Croque Monsieur".

Marinaded, Roasted Chicken Pieces with Green Beans

If you're having a fair number of hearty eaters to cater for, you can make the Beans the day before (see recipe on page 182). To complete a healthy repast, serve them with marinaded, roasted chicken pieces and roast potatoes, which need not be of the "grease bomb" variety.

A few hours before the meal, put the chicken pieces (one for each person) in a large roasting tin and sprinkle with some olive oil, a teaspoon each of cumin, cinnamon and garlic powder, salt and pepper and a cup of red wine. Toss around to cover all the pieces with the marinade. Set aside.

Peel the spuds and put in another roasting tray. Toss in a table spoon of olive oil and swirl the spuds round in it. Stick them in a hot oven for around an hour. After 20 minutes put the chicken into the oven. At the end of the hour everything should be ready.

Some village bread, warmed on the oven for a few minutes and a salad and you ought to fill 'em up!

Kolokassi Cassoulet

Ingredients for 6 servings

1 k lean chicken, lamb or pork fillet
  cut into 4cm chunks
2 medium onions, peeled and finely chopped
1-2 sticks of celery, chopped
6 medium tomatoes, skinned and well chopped
2 tbsp of tomato purée

100 ml of lemon juice
1 k or a little more of kolokassi
250 ml of meat or chicken stock or water with stock cube
6 tbsp of oil for frying
Salt and pepper to taste

Method

* In your frying pan heat half the oil and quickly brown the meat on all sides. Turn down the heat and cook for around 10 minutes. Remove from the pan and put into a large saucepan.
* Peel the kolokassi and wipe it dry. Do not wash it, as it becomes slimy. Cut it into small pieces by cutting it lengthwise and then across (some Cypriot cooks say it is better to pierce the kolokassi with the point of a kitchen knife and break it into pieces, because it takes longer to cook if cut with a knife and this could be important if you are using tender, quick-cooking meat).
* Heat the remaining oil in the frying pan and gently fry the onion and celery for around 5 minutes.
* Add the kolokassi and continue cooking for a further 5 minutes, stirring regularly.
* Remove the mixture from the pan and add to the meat.
* Add the tomatoes, tomato purée and lemon juice and stir in gently. Season to taste.
* Cover the mixture with the stock and simmer until the meat and the kolokassi are cooked through. Stir carefully from time to time.

As a variation, the tomatoes may be omitted and the amount of stock increased. Another way of cooking this dish is simply to put all the ingredients in a large casserole and bake the dish in the oven.

Sikitakia Peri-Peri   (A peppery Portuguese dish)

Ingredients (serves 4-6 as a starter)

500 g chicken livers, cleaned and trimmed
200 g of peeled chopped tomatoes
1 large onion, peeled and shredded
1 clove of garlic, crushed
A pinch of Cayenne pepper or 4 fresh, de-seeded chopped chilis
3 or 4 cloves
A small cinnamon stick

Method

*   Sauté the onions in a little oil or clarified butter until golden brown.
*   Add the chopped tomatoes, together with the crushed clove of garlic.
*   Add the finely chopped chilis or pinch of Cayenne pepper, the cloves and the small cinnamon stick.
*   Bring to the boil and then reduce on a low heat for about 30 minutes.
*   In a little oil or clarified butter, cook the livers very quickly, sealing them on both sides (so they are still pink in the middle).
*   Flare with a little brandy.
*   Pour the livers and juices into the pan and cook for another 10 minutes on a low heat.

Chicken, Courgette and Ham Pie

Ingredients for 4 servings

2 cooked chicken breasts, chopped into small chunks
1 340g (12 oz) packet of Jus Rol puff pastry, defrosted
and rolled out to approximately four times its area
1 large onion, peeled and finely sliced
2-3 smallish courgettes
5 slices of lounza or back bacon, finely sliced

1 cup of grated **Cheddar** or Cyprus Tilsit cheese
2 tbsp of flour
2 or 3 cups of milk
Salt and pepper
A sprinkling of garlic powder

Method

* Roll out the pastry, cut into four pieces, brush with beaten egg or milk and bake in a hot oven (225°C) for about 15-20 minutes or until you see that it is cooked through.
* Take a slice of butter about ⅛th of a packet and melt in your non-stick frying pan until it is sizzling.
* Fry the onion and the bacon until they are beginning to brown.
* Turn down the heat and add the chopped courgettes. Cook for 4-5 minutes.
* Sprinkle the flour over the mixture, stir in and continue frying, stirring all the time.
* Slowly pour in the milk, mixing well to form a sauce of a thick, creamy consistency. Add more milk as necessary.
* After a few minutes, put in the chicken chunks.
* Grate the cheese and stir into the sauce, and simmer very slowly until it is melted.
* Take the four pastry pieces and, with a sharp knife, cut open from the side.
* Spoon the sauce mixture onto the bottom half of the pastry, cover with the top and bring to the table.

Drink a bottle of young, fruity red with this and all will be well with the world.

Salads

Salads

Broad Beans

Broad beans are lovely in salads.

* Drop the potatoes from a **Salade Niçoise** and substitute tiny raw or blanched small fresh or frozen broad beans.
* Make a delicious **Salade Tiède:** Grill bacon until crisp, chop and add to warm broad beans, finely shredded raw red cabbage, lettuce, cucumber and spring onions. Toss in a French dressing and serve at once.
* Slice **cold pork sausages**, add to cooked broad beans, thinly sliced green and red peppers and onion rings. Add an oil and lemon dressing to which a teaspoon of tomato purée has been stirred in.

Warm Broad Bean & Bacon Salad

Ingredients for 6
1 450 g packet of good small frozen broad beans
6-8 rashers of bacon
1 large onion, peeled and sliced
1 tomato, peeled and deseeded

Juice of 1 lemon
2 tbsp salad oil
A tiny drop of vinegar
Salt and pepper
Sprig parsley, finely chopped

Method
* Place the frozen broad beans in a shallow pan and pour boiling water over them. Quickly bring them back to the boil, then drain and put them in a bowl. If they are small, you need only "show" them the boiling water.
* Fry the bacon until crisp. Remove from the pan, chop into thin strips and add to the broad beans.
* Add the onion and tomato to the bowl.
* Finally, add the finely chopped parsley. Dribble over the salad oil, the lemon juice, a tiny drop of vinegar, salt and pepper.
* Mix everything together and serve.

Chick Pea & Tomato Salad

Ingredients (for 4-6 servings)

400 g can of chick peas, drained
1 large onion
3-4 medium-large tomatoes
1 large clove of garlic (optional)
Half tsp of powdered cumin
2 tbsp olive oil
Salt and pepper

Method

* Peel and very finely slice the onion and garlic.
* In a frying pan, cook the onion and garlic quite slowly until they begin to brown and crispen (around 15-20 minutes).
* Add the cumin, stir and carry on frying for a minute or so.
* Peel and de-seed the tomatoes, then chop into thin slices and add them to the pan. Cook slowly for 2-3 minutes.
* Drain the chick peas and add to the pan. Stir and cook for a further 2-3 minutes.

Serve warm, or leave to cool, in which case some lemon juice and chopped mint may be added.

Fattoush

Ingredients (for 4-6 servings)

1 piece of Arab or Pitta bread	1 tbsp mint, 1 tbsp parsley, finely chopped
The inside leaves of a lettuce	4 tbsp salad oil
4-5 medium-sized tomatoes, skinned	Juice of 1 large lemon
1 bunch of salad onions	1 crushed garlic clove
1 small green or red pepper	Salt and pepper
2 Cyprus cucumbers, peeled.	

Method

* Toast or oven-bake the bread until it is dry but not too crisp. Cut or break into small pieces or strips.
* Shred the lettuce into very fine strips
* De-seed and slice pepper very, very thinly
* Trim and finely slice spring onions.
* Remove skins and chop tomatoes and cucumbers.
* Put all ingredients except the bread into a salad bowl, mix and season with salt and pepper to taste.
* Just before serving, add the bread.

Fattoush is a nice light dish on its own, or accompanying cold meats, ham, salami or grilled fish. Some chefs now fry the small strips of bread, instead of toasting, which adds a little extra flavour.

Tabbouleh

The secret of this dish is to chop everything very finely. You will need ....

At least 2 bunches of parsley
4 large salad onions (scallions) with as much of the green part as possible
4 good sprigs of fresh mint
75 g (half a teacup) of medium grain Bulgar Wheat (Pourgourri)

2 large tomatoes, skinned, de-seeded and diced very small
2 tbsp of lemon juice
2 tbsp of olive oil
Salt and pepper

Method

* Wash the parsley very well. Drain, shake and chop very finely.
* In a small bowl, soak the Bulgar Wheat (Pourgourri) in water for 2 minutes. Drain and set aside.
* Add the finely chopped parsley to the Bulgar Wheat.
* Chop the spring onions very finely and add.
* Finally, put in the finely chopped tomatoes, well drained, and add salt and pepper, lemon juice and olive oil.
* Stir well.

On a large serving dish place a number of fresh heart-of-lettuce leaves. Put the Tabbouleh in the centre of the lettuce leaves and serve at once.

It is ideal with barbecued or grilled meats.

"La Dolce Vita" Warm Spaghetti Salad

It is said that this is popular with the smarter citizens of Rome for lunch on hot summer days. It adapts ideally to Cypriot ingredients and is simple and inexpensive to make.

Ingredients (serves 4)

450 g peeled, de-seeded and chopped tomatoes
125 g halloumi, chopped into small cubes
4-6 anchovy fillets, chopped
1 des-sp capers (briefly washed)
Finely chopped or crushed garlic to taste

2 tbsp olive oil
A good handful of plump pitted black olives
Fresh basil leaves, hand-broken
Salt and pepper
350 g spaghetti

Method

* Put all the ingredients, except the spaghetti, into a large bowl and mix together well.
* In a large saucepan, cook the spaghetti in plenty of salted boiling water, according to instructions on the packet.
* When ready, drain and mix into the salad mixture and serve at once.

Accompaniments

If the day is hot, I would serve this dish with sliced cucumbers tossed in oil, lemon and finely ground mint and a chopped green salad of lettuce, lachana, green pepper and some parsley. Then some crusty fresh bread and a cool glass of dry rosé wine.

Hiromeri & Artichoke Salad
Ingredients for 6-8 portions

450 g of Cyprus 'Tricolore' Pasta Twists
150 g of very thinly sliced Hiromeri
1 can of artichoke hearts, sliced
1 cup of stoned black olives
3-4 tsp Cyprus capers, coarsely chopped
Dressing (see below)

Method

*   In a large pan, cook the pasta until almost tender in boiling water with a coffee spoon of salt.
*   Drain well and turn into a good sized dish, sprinkle over a little oil and stir.
*   Slice the Hiromeri into strips and add to the pasta, along with the chopped artichoke hearts, the pitted olives and capers.
*   Make a dressing from a coffee cup of your preferred salad oil (I like a light olive oil), a tablespoonful of wine vinegar, a good teaspoon of made mustard, salt and pepper to taste, and stir into the pasta.
*   Sprinkle with chopped parsley and serve, with crusty bread.

And if you want a side salad to complement this very tasty offering: a green one, perhaps? Simply: washed, dried, heart-of-lettuce leaves; peeled and very thinly sliced cucumbers and finely chopped salad onions - with a light dressing of a little oil and lemon and a hint of garlic.

Quite light it may be, but I like a fairly robust red wine with this dish.

Oriental Salad (for six people)

Ingredients for the salad

1 420 g can of bean sprouts, very well drained
A wedge of cabbage, finely sliced
1 green pepper, de-seeded and thinly sliced
2 Cyprus cucumbers, peeled and thinly sliced
1 medium-large carrot, coarsley grated

Ingredients for the Dressing

1 tsp soy sauce
1 scant tsp ginger/garlic/pepper sauce or half
 tsp each of ground ginger, powdered garlic and
 a pinch or two of chili pepper
4 tbsp salad oil
1 tps caster sugar
Black pepper
1 tbsp rice wine vinegar or white wine vinegar

Method

*   Toss all the salad ingredients in a large bowl.

To make the dressing, if you have a small blender, simply put all the ingredients in and whizz for a few seconds.

Otherwise...
*   In a cup or small bowl, mix the sugar, soy sauce and spices and mix with a fork or small whisk.
*   Mix in the vinegar and pepper.
*   Lastly, add the oil, little by little, and blend thoroughly.
*   Throw over the salad, toss and serve with griddled Pitta bread. (Pitta, brushed with a little oil and briefly sizzled each side on a griddle on high heat)

Caesar Salad

Californian cuisine is fast-moving, ecletic and international—every imaginable combination of ingredients can be found. Like this funny gooey old salad, alleged to have crept across the border from Mexico.

Ingredients (6-8 servings as a starter)

4 tbsp olive oil, or preferred light oil for cooking and 4 tbsp for salad

4 thick slices of dry white bread, crusts removed and cut into cubes

2 medium sized lettuce, tough green outside leaves removed

2 medium cloves garlic, peeled and coarsely chopped

1 egg

2 small cans of anchovy fillets, oil removed, separated and cut into halves.

1 heaped tbsp Parmesan or other hard cheese, plus lemon juice, salt and pepper

Method

* Wash and dry the lettuce and put in fridge for 1 hour
* In a sturdy frying pan, heat oil. Fry garlic and the bread cubes until golden brown on all sides ("Big croutons"!)
* Remove croutons, dry on kitchen paper, set aside. Discard garlic and oil from pan.
* Slice lettuce, and put in a large bowl, round which you have rubbed a garlic clove.
* Pour in 4 tbsp olive oil and toss lettuce very well indeed.
* Boil egg for just one minute. Break it over the lettuce and mix.
* Separate and cut in half the anchovy fillets and add to salad with 2 tsp lemon juice, freshly ground black pepper, salt to taste and the grated cheese.
* Toss with style and panache (i.e. enthusiastically) to thoroughly coat the lettuce with lovely, gooey mixture.
* Just before serving add your golden crispy croutons, mix in and whip onto the table as a super starter.

Cooked Lentil Salad

Cooked lentils make an excellent salad ingredient.
*   Soak a cupful overnight, drain and simmer in 75 cl of water until tender.
*   Cool and add to chopped onions, tomatoes, sliced **Lounza** and a few cooked peas (or anything else you fancy) for colour.
*   Dress with oil and lemon juice and serve with hot Pitta bread.

"Ton e Fagioli"

Ingredients

400 g can of red kidney beans (drained)
200 g can of tuna steak
Some spring onions
A drop of lemon juice
Seasoning

Method
*   Chop the onions and put into a bowl with the tuna (and its oil) and the beans.
*   Add lemon juice and more oil if you wish.
*   Season.

If you want to use fresh green beans instead of red kidney beans, you can ... Just cook 500 g or so, chop, cool and proceed as above. The only difference then is that you've got "Ton e Fagiolini".

Salad Dressings

There are two ways of doing this. The first is popular around the Mediterranean region: you make your salad and then you sprinkle over it some oil, some vinegar or lemon juice, some salt and pepper and toss the salad. Oil and vinegar/lemon are usually in proportions of three parts oil to one part vinegar/lemon. The second is to make a dressing, usually undertaken by less lazy cooks and better restaurants, again using three parts oil to one part vinegar. The oil you use accords to the taste you want – the more robust dressings use extra virgin olive oil, the blander ones use sunflower or ground-nut. After that, you go on to add all kinds of flavourings according to your wishes and whims. You may add herbs, a little spice, some sugar, tomato juice, mustard, honey, even a dab of chicken stock as in the recipe for the classic *Salade Niçoise*.

Then there are vinegars. Most dressings use wine vinegar, red or white. But there is excellent sherry vinegar and flavoured wine vinegars: raspberry, tarragon, thyme, sage, to name but a few. Start out with a simple 3-to-1 oil and vinegar dressing and go on from there. Here is one excellent example, from my friend with an English farmhouse, John Diebel.

Diebel's Drizzling Dressing

In a small bowl put:
25 cl of good olive oil
1 des-sp of John's home-made honey (Cyprus honey would do)
1 des-sp of white wine vinegar
1 good tsp of Dijon mustard
Salt and pepper to taste

Drizzle over your salad and toss. The honey makes it!

Rice
and
Pulses

Rice & Pulses

Rice - General

An American-Italian cookery book in my possession tells me that Italy is the largest rice growing country in Europe, producing "about" 1 million tonnes a year. This seeems pretty impressive, until you realise that the only other countries in Europe, which grow any at all are Spain, France and Poruga and that a country like Sri Lanka grows about 6 million.

The rice fields of this world produce an estimated total of around 480 million tonnes annually or something like 350 million of rice that is ready to cook. Of course, there are also many varieities of plant and different methods of processing. For most of us the rice we use for savoury recipes is medium or long grain, whilst short grain is used in puddings. But in the Far East, particularly in Japan, short grain rice that comes out decidely gelatinous is preferred. In Cyprus, probably the most used are American long-grain and Indian Basmati., whilst the nearest rice-growing countries are Egypt and Turkey.

I am sometimes asked how to cook rice and I have to admit I have not made a detailed study of the various types of rice and their cookery. For the every day cook, it depends on what sort of result you like. Some people like a rather wet, gelatinous result, whilst others, like me, prefer a dry, slightly nutty finish with every grain separate.

In the first case you may use 3-4 cups of water to each cup or rice and simply drain off any excess water when the rice is done to your satisfaction. My preferred method is to pour water or stock into a pan to the level of cooked rice you would like, bring to the boil and quickly pour in the rice (American long-grain, unwashed) until it just comes in a pyramid to the surface of the liquid. Bring back to the boil, put the lid on and simmer for 20 minutes and you should have perfectly cooked , separate grain, rice.

An advantage of the "separate grain" method is that cooked rice can be used in salads to considerable effect.

Levant Pilaff

Ingredients for 4

500 g of lamb chops
1 turkey or 2 cooked chicken breasts, sliced
1 coffee cup of pinolia (pine kernels) or almond pieces
2 medium-large onions
1 clove of garlic

2 flat tsp cinnamon
1 flat tsp cumin
Chicken or turkey stock
Rice Pilaff (see next page)

Method

* If frozen, de-frost the chops. Remove meat and fat and mince or grind quite coarsely. Set bones aside for stock.
* Finely chop the onion and garlic.
* In a frying pan or skillet melt a walnut-sized knob of butter and fry the pinolia or almonds until beginning to brown. Stir regularly.
* Add the minced/ground lamb and continue frying and stirring. When the juices are evaporating and the meat is browning, add the onions and garlic and continue cooking for around 10 minutes.
* Add the spices, salt and pepper to taste and stir. Keep cooking on a low heat. If the mixture gets dry, add some stock.
* Cook until the lamb is tender. Remove from the stove.
* Make the pilaff (see next recipe). Warm cooked chicken or turkey breast slices in a little stock.
* On a large oval platter, turn out the pilaff. Make an indent in the centre and put in the lamb mixture. Place the hot chicken or turkey slices around the edge and serve.

Pilaff for 4 or more

Ingredients

500 g of pilaff or long grain rice
Chicken or turkey stock (1 l or more)
125 g (1 cup) of short fine pasta (Vermicellini - very thin)
A knob of butter

Method

*   In a large pan, melt the butter.
*   When sizzling, pour in the little short strands of pasta and stir until it is going brown.
*   Pour in the stock and bring to the boil.
*   Pour in the rice until it makes a mound and touches the surface of the stock, stir.
*   Cover and cook slowly for around 20 minutes or until the rice is tender. Add more stock if necessary to make a nice, rich juicy pilaff.

Moulded Rice with Lahana

This dish can look absolutely stunning but requires a little bit of care in the making.

Ingredients

300 g of lahana (Swiss Chard), trimmed of choggy bits and chopped
2 tbsp olive oil
1 large onion, very finely chopped
90 g of butter
Salt
180 g of button mushrooms, sliced, or 6 small rashers
of streaky bacon
450 g of rice. The Italians recommend Arborio but, if this is not obtainable, one that produces a slightly glutinous result.
120 g freshly grated hard cheese. Fresh Parmesan is ideal, but otherwise a local hard cheese such as dry Anari.

Method
*   In a large pan, cook the lahana in boiling salted water for about five minutes. Drain in a colander and leave for as much liquid as possible to drain. Then chop it finely and sauté in the olive oil for five minutes.
*   Remove from the frying pan and fry the chopped onion in the butter until it is beginning to brown. Add the mushrooms or bacon and cook for a few minutes over a moderate heat.
*   In a large stew pan, put about 1.5 l of water with some salt, bring to the boil and add the rice. When this comes to the boil, turn down the heat, stir once to settle, cover and simmer for about 15 minutes. Do not stir again.

Moulded Rice with Lahana (continued)

*   If there is liquid remaining with the rice, drain it, then transfer the rice to a large bowl, adding the mushroom or bacon mixture and the grated cheese. Mix very well.
*   Now generously rub the sides and the bottom of the ring mould with butter. Fill it with the rice mixture and press down firmly and carefully. In a pre-heated oven at 200°C, bake for about 30 minutes. The trick is to get the outside of the rice mould golden brown and this will depend on the type of rice you use and how glutinous it is. I'm afraid that a little trial and error is the only possibility!
*   When you think it is ready (and to see, you take out the mould and peek with knife at the edge) decant the rice onto a large serving dish, brown side upwards.
*   Finally, having kept the lahana warm, carefully place it in the middle of the mould and serve.

The mushroom-based variety could be served with Sauté of Chicken, Fried Chicken Escalopes or Pork Fillet. The bacon-flavoured job is ideally served with a tomato sauce.

Left-overs of the mould don't present a problem. Break 'em up, slap in some stir-fried vegetables/chicken/ham/anything you like, and you've got a splendid risotto. Or, cold, you can chop in onion, tomato, cucumber, shredded cabbage, cold peas and so on.

Spicy Risotto

Ingredients

Enough cooked chicken for four people
1 large onion, finely shredded
3 garlic cloves, finely chopped
200 g of button mushrooms, finely sliced
1 tsp each of powdered ginger, powdered cumin,
powdered cinnamon, turmeric

Half tsp (or more, if you wish) of ground red pepper
100 g (a scant teacupful) of almonds, blanched, peeled
and coarsely chopped
A generous grinding of freshly milled black pepper
450 g Basmati rice
1 l chicken stock

Method

* First boil your rice in the stock (1 measure of rice to 3 measures of liquid).
* In a good sized frying pan, put 2 tbsp of olive oil and fry the onion until it is beginning to brown at the edges.
* Add the garlic, chopped almonds and sliced mushrooms and stir-fry for about 5 minutes.
* Add the cooked chicken and all the spices.
* Keep on frying, stirring regularly for about 10 minutes; then add about 3 tbsp of chicken stock. Stir in, lower the heat and simmer for a few minutes.
* Stir in the cooked rice, put a lid on and, on a very low heat, cook for a further 5 minutes.
* Serve with yogurt, mango chutney and a salad of finely chopped onions and peeled and sliced tomatoes, with a sprinkling of black pepper, salt and paprika. A green salad on the side, some Arabic or Indian bread and, if you can find one, a genuine dry rosé wine.

Suleiman's Pilaff

Ingredients

450 g long-grain rice
1 l light meat or chicken stock
450 g of cooked lamb, diced
2 good sized onions and 2 cloves garlic, finely sliced
450 g of ripe tomatoes, peeled and chopped
1 coffee cup of pine-nuts or sliced peeled almonds,
   grilled brown

60 g currants or sultanas
5-6 tbsp rendered lamb fat, "dripping" or olive oil
1 scant tsp ground cinnamon and 2 pinches ground
cumin
Salt and pepper to taste

Method

*   In a heavy saucepan with lid, heat 4 tbsp of fat or oil, tip in the rice and stir well until rice has a coating of fat.
*   Pour in the stock, cover and bring to boil. Turn down the heat and put lid on. After 15-20 minutes the rice should be cooked and the liquid absorbed.
*   In a large frying pan, heat the remainder of the fat/oil and fry onions until beginning to turn golden.
*   Add all the other ingredients and gently fry for 5-8 minutes.
*   Combine the meat mixture and the rice in a large warmed serving bowl and dish up with yogurt and salad.

And what, pray can one do with cooked rice, when there's no meat about? Veggie pilaffs can be delicious—the next recipe for instance...

Vegetable Pilaffery

One   Onions, very, very thinly sliced, fried in a very little oil, very slowly, until they are going brown and crisp; add some flaked almonds and thinly sliced mushrooms, stir and fry for another five minutes or so. Mix in the rice and serve.

Two   Just as the rice is cooked, stir in frozen peas, sweet corn and very finely sliced red pepper and leave for 5-10 minutes. Very pretty.

Three   "Suleiman's Pilaff" without the meat. Slice and fry an onion and several cloves of garlic. When they are on the turn add a sliced green pepper, some mushrooms and a handful of sultanas, and fry for 5 more minutes. Then stir in 3-4 chopped tomatoes. Cook on medium heat for around 10 minutes, adding salt, pepper, powdered cumin and cinnamon to taste. Serve on a bed of rice.

Pourgourri Pilaff

Ingredients

200 grams of coarse Bulgar Wheat (Pourgourri or Burghul)
50 grams of very fine noodles (Vermicellini), crushed very small
25 cl of tomato juice
75 cl of water (a full wine bottle)
1 small onion, sliced very finely
3 tablespoons of oil
Juice of half a lemon
Salt and pepper to taste

Method

*   Heat the oil in a saucepan and fry the onion.
*   When the onion is transparent, add the noodles and fry, stirring constantly until they start to brown. Be careful not to burn them.
*   Add the water, tomato juice and lemon juice and bring to the boil.
*   Put in the Bulgar Wheat, stir, season to taste, reduce heat and simmer very gently with the pan lid on until the liquid is absorbed.
*   Taste to see that the pilaff is cooked and, if it is not, add a little more water.

As a side dish to grills, this pilaff is delicious. Yogurt or Tsatsiki (yogurt and cucumber salad – see page 58) are also an excellent accompaniment.

Lentils, Cyprus Style

Within the walls of Nicosia, not in the tourist section, you can still find little cafés where Mama cooks and Papa serves (or vice versa), in which you can find four, five, six pots on the stove, each one contsaining a traditional, pre-prosperity Cyprus dish and now scorned by most. They should be preserved, because they are great. This is my version of one of them.

Ingredients

450 grams of "green" lentils
1 largish onion, peeled and finely chopped
2 medium carrots, peeled and coarsely chopped
2-3 sticks of celery, thinly sliced
2 cloves garlic, peeled and chopped
50 cl chicken or vegetable stock

Method

* Wash lentils in a sieve, then put them in a pot and cover them with water. Bring to boil and cook.
* When tender, drain and set aside.
* In a good-sized stewpan, stir-fry the vegetables in olive oil for 5 minutes. Put in a little stock, cover and sikmer until tender.
* Add lentils and remainder of stock, stir and simmer for a few minutes and then serve.

Very nice as a main dish with fresh bread and salad or as an accompaniment to roast or grilled meat or fish.

Vegetables

Black Eye Beans & Lahana

Ingredients

370 g [2 cups] dried black eye beans, soaked overnight
2 medium onions
1 bunch of Lahana (Swiss Chard)
Juice of one lemon
1 large garlic clove
2-3 tbsp olive oil
Salt and pepper to taste

Method

* Drain the black eye beans and place in a pan of boiling water and cook until tender (45-60 minutes)
* Peel and very finely slice the onion, and finely chop garlic.
* Put the oil in a pan, heat and quite quickly fry the onion and garlic until crisp and brown at the edges. Set aside
* Chop Lahana into thick strips, including stalks and place in a saucepan with a little boiling water. Cover and cook until reasonably tender (don't overdo it!) When cooked, drain and add the lemon juice and salt and pepper.
* Combine the black eye beans, the lahana, onion and garlic and stir. Serve warm, or cool and serve with a little more oil and lemon dribbled over it, with some chopped parsley on top.

Celery & Peas

You'll need half a head of celery, washed and chopped into short pieces, a good knob of butter, 2 cupfuls of frozen peas and a large cup of stock.

In a medium sized stewpan, melt the butter. On a medium heat, put in the chopped celery and stir-fry for a couple of minutes. Turn down the heat and cover the pan, letting the celery cook for around ten minutes. Make sure it doesn 't go dry. Then add the stock and cook until celery is almost tender. Add the peas and simmer for 10-15 minutes until peas are tender. Serve.

Courgettes alla Romana

Slice some courgettes, dip in your own favourite batter mixture and deep fry in hot oil. Serve with a hot tomato sauce (chopped onion, garlic clove and peeled tomatoes, salt and pepper and a bay leaf fried in a tablespoon or two of olive oil). (See recipe page 35.)

Courgettes with Garlic & Parsely

Take four courgettes and coarsely grate them. Very finely chop two cloves of garlic and 2-3 good sprigs of parsley. Add to the grated courgettes and mix in. Sprinkle with salt and pepper and mix.

Melt a knob or two of butter in a frying pan on high heat. Add the courgette mixture and stir-fry for 2 minutes. Do not let courgettes get sloshy. Serve at once.

Courgettes with Onions, Tomatoes & Potatoes

Courgettes bake well with onions, tomatoes and potatoes, in this Greek dish which is great for lunch or dinner parties because it can be kept a while in a warm oven until you're ready to serve it. It'll make a meatless main dish, too. For a generous tray, take

1 kilo of potatoes, peeled and chopped into chunks
750 g of courgettes, sliced across
2-3 large onions, peeled and sliced
3-4 garlic cloves, peeled and chopped
500 g tomatoes, skinned and chopped into chunks
Salt and pepper and chopped fresh herbs of your choice.

Method

* Pour 4-5 tbsp of olive oil into a large baking dish and put all the ingredients in.
* Mix well together with the oil and bake in a hot oven (200°C) for 45-60 minutes.
* Stir once or twice during this time.

Fasolia

Fasolia is not difficult to make. Seasonally, you can find the "fresh" haricot beans in the shops—long pods looking rather dry. Unfortunately, they're expensive, too, but worth it for a treat. Remove the beans and cook until almost tender, not only for "Fasolia" but salads and many other dishes.

Or, you can use dry white beans, soaked for 24 hours, then rinsed and put back into a pan of water. Bring to the boil, skim, change the water and bring back to the boil, cover and cook slowly for 2-3 hours, until tender. Reserve liquid.
Or, you can use two 400 g cans of Cannellini beans, reserving the juice, for the following recipe, which will feed eight:

Ingredients

500 g of cooked white beans
Half a head of celery
3-4 carrots
4 medium onions

2 large cloves of garlic
4 medium-large tomatoes, skins removed.
4-5 tbsp olive oil
Salt, or one vegetable stock cube and pepper

Method

*   In a large stewpan heat the olive oil. When hot, tip in the celery, carrots and onion and stir round.
*   Keep on high heat, stirring regularly, for five minutes.
*   Turn heat to low and cover the pan. Stir every few minutes and simmer gently for about 15 minutes.
*   When the vegetables are tender, add the tomatoes and the beans, with the juice and carry on cooking slowly. Add salt or crumbled stock cubes, and pepper to taste and stir in.
*   Add a little water if necessary. After 15 minutes this staple Cyprus dish is ready to serve, but you can gently simmer it for longer if you like. Its flavour develops over a day and it keeps for several days in the fridge.

Jansson's Temptation (an old Swedish favourite)

Ingredients

6 - 8 medium-large potatoes, peeled
2 medium onions
3 tbsp unsalted butter

200 g of Swedish canned Anchovy fillets (Ansjovis Filéer)
27 cl of light cream
Black pepper

Method

* Heat the oven to 200°C
* Cut potatoes into slices about 5mm thick, then cut each slice into 5mm wide sticks
* Peel and slice the onions
* Gently fry the onions in half the butter until transparent
* Unleash the Ansjovis from the can, drain and keep the liquid
* Line the bottom of an oven dish or baking try with a layer of the potatoes. Then put a layer of onion and one of Ansjovis. Make a top layer of potato.
* Dot the top with the remaining butter and grind some black pepper over. Dribble over the liquid from the Ansjovis and half of the cream.
* Bake in the oven for around 20 minutes. Remove and pour over the remaining cream and bake for a further half hour or until the potatoes are cooked through, but not slushy.

NOTE: whatever you do, if you can't find SWEDISH Ansjovis, do not use Spanish, Greek or Portuguese Anchovy fillets. Instead use a jar of "Abbas" Herring in Dill or Onion, or Marinaded Salmon (Gravad Lax), which is available in most large supermarkets.

Leeks Provençal *Hot or cold – a delicious dish for your Mezedes*

Ingredients for 4 Servings

-3 medium sized leeks, carefully washed
and chopped into thickish rings.
A modest amount of water for cooking
1 tbsp of olive oil
1 tbsp tomato purée

2 tsp lemon juice
25 cl of water or chicken stock
A few drops of white wine vinegar
Salt and pepper to taste

Method

* Simmer leeks in water barely covering them until almost tender. Drain and remove from pan.
* Heat olive oil and stir in tomato purée and cook for a minute or two.
* Pour in cup of water or stock, stir well, return to stove and reduce by about half.
* Put back the leeks. Add lemon juice, salt and pepper, stir and cook gently for about a minute.
* Remove from heat, sprinkle a few drops of vinegar over leeks and stir.

Peperonata

* Wash and de-seed 6-8 large red, green and yellow peppers and cut into thick strips.
* Heat 4 tbsp of olive oil in a large frying pan and fry the sliced peppers with 4 large skinned and chopped tomatoes, 3-4 crushed cloves of garlic and a couple of large pinches of oregano.
* Cover the pan and cook on a very low heat for 40-45 minutes.
* Add salt and pepper to taste. Serve hot or cold.

Patates Yiahni

Ingredients

1 k of small potatoes, cleaned and peeled
3 good sized really red Cyprus cooking tomatoes, skinned
1 large onion, peeled and thinly sliced
250 ml of olive oil
750 ml of water
Salt and pepper and a tiny scrap of a fresh herb of your choice if you like.

Method

*   Heat the oil in a large saucepan and fry the onion until it has become transparent (not brown).
*   Add the tomatoes and cook for 5-10 minutes on a high heat, stirring regularly. Add herb if you wish.
*   Add the potatoes and cook well for 5 minutes, stirring regularly.
*   Add 750 ml of water and bring to boiling.
*   Turn stove down to medium and cook briskly until potatoes are well cooked and the sauce is quite thick.

What, no garlic?

Well, of course you could add a clove or two and fry with the onions. You can also cook lots of other vegetables in the oil-onion-tomato base—celery and peas; peas and artichoke hearts; carrots and celery ... and so forth.

Rosti Potatoes

Rosti potatoes are an excellent accompaniment to cold meats.
Easy to make, especially if you have two non-stick frying pans the same size.

Ingredients

450 g potatoes
3 tbsp frying oil
1 medium onion, finely chopped
Salt and pepper

Method

*   Boil the potatoes in their skins until cooked through but not soft.
*   Cool and remove skins. Grate coarsely.
*   Fry the onion in the oil until it begins to brown.
*   Gently stir in the potatoes, spreading evenly over the pan and cook on a medium heat for about ten minutes.
*   Next you have to turn the Rosti over to cook the other side for ten minutes. You can slide it on to a plate if
        you like and put the frying pan, inverted over it, and then transfer it, or you can simply use a second pan and
        flip it over.

Serve straight from the pan, garnished with chopped parsley.
Another version, which I also like uses grated raw potato and onion mixed, which should be cooked slightly more slowly.
You may also add 1 tbsp of flour and an egg to raw grated potatoes, mix well, and fry quite slowly, which gives you the
taste of both fried potato and batter. Fattening, but exquisite.

Spinach & Rice (Serves 6)

Ingredients

1 k of spinach, washed, dried and finely chopped
2 medium onions or 6 spring onions, finely sliced
250 g of rice
25 cl of olive or sunflower oil
1.5 l water
Salt and freshly ground black pepper

Method

* Heat oil in a heavy saucepan and fry onions until transparent.
* Add spinach and stir-fry for a minute or two
* Tip in three cups of water and boil for about 4-5 minutes until spinach is almost cooked.
* Add remaining water, bring to boil and put in the rice.
* Salt and pepper, cover pan and simmer until water is absorbed and rice is cooked.

Different cooks add various flavourings: a tiny drop of chopped mint or dill in the cooking, a sprinkling of cinnamon or ground coriander seeds and, at the serving, lemon juice.

Stir-fried Vegetables
You can stir fry almost any combination of fresh vegetables. For example:

Ingredients

50 g of small florets of broccoli or cauliflower
2-3 salad onions sliced
50 g carrots, sliced very fine
Half celery stick sliced very, very fine
60g of de-frosted frozen peas
125g of bean sprouts, fresh or canned

25 cl of chicken or vegetable stock
1 tbsp soy sauce
Half tsp of sugar
2 tsp of cornflour
Black pepper

Method

* Mix the cooled stock, soy sauce, sugar and several grindings of black pepper. Have the cornflour to hand.
* If using canned beansprouts, drain **thoroughly**, getting them as dry as possible.
* Heat a wok or non-stick frying pan, add 2 tablespoons of sunflower or ground-nut oil and when very hot, add all the vegetables, *except the bean sprouts*.
* Vigorously fry on high heat, stirring constantly for a couple of minutes. Add the beansprouts and stir in.
* Tip the cornflour into a little of the stock and mix well.
* Add remainder of stock, stir and tip into the vegetables.
* Cook for a further minute stirring all the time. Serve.

This dish is splendid with fried or grilled fillets of steak, chicken or fish, and/or with noodles.

Yemistes - Stuffed Vegetables

You can stuff many vegetables, but the favourites must be green peppers, tomatoes, courgettes and onions.

There are many variations of stuffing. All use rice, adding meat, vegetables, pine-nuts, herbs and whatever. Here is a meat recipe sufficient for 12 pieces.

The first thing to do is to prepare the vegetables. Cut the tops off the tomatoes and gently remove most of the flesh from inside them, taking care not to pierce the skin. Discard the seeds. Cut the top off the peppers and remove the core and seeds.

Keep the tops of the tomatoes and peppers.

After cutting one end off, with a long thin sharp knife or apple corer, remove the centre of the courgettes or aubergines. Set aside with flesh of the tomatoes.

If stuffing large onions, microwave or simmer until almost tender and gently remove the inside with a sharp knife.

The tricky bit is over ... on to the stuffing mixture, as follows. Basically, you're making a good rich mince.

Ingredients
450 g of finely minced lean lamb (for me it can only be lamb)
2 medium onions and 1 large clove garlic, finely chopped
Flesh from inside of the vegetables
Chopped mint and parsley or oregano and thyme, as you like
80 g long-grain rice
Half tsp sugar
4-5 tbsp olive oil
250 ml stock and a little tomato purée
Salt and pepper

Continued on next page.

Yemistes continued.

Method

* Heat the oven to 190°C
* In a large frying pan, heat 3-4 tbsp of the oil, and fry the chopped onions and garlic until starting to brown.
* Add minced meat, stir in and fry, turning regularly, until juices have disappeared and meat is browning. Add the herbs, tomato, courgette or aubergine pulp and cook for 5-6 minutes, stirring regularly.
* Add stock and tsp of tomato purée, season to taste. Carry on simmering, checking liquid, now and then adding a little more stock if necessary.
* After about half an hour, when the meat should be tender, add the rice and cook gently for a few minutes until rice becomes shiny. Remove from stove.
* Sprinkle a little sugar into the inside of each tomato, pepper, etc and spoon in the stuffing, filling about three-quarters of each piece, leaving space for the rice to expand. Put the 'lids' on and place in a baking tray.
* Drizzle a little oil over each one. Pour a cup of stock or seasoned water into the tray and cover it with aluminium foil. *(Remove this after 45 minutes of baking.)*
* Bake for about 90 minutes in a medium oven (190°C) or until the rice is tender.
* Serve with roast potatoes and a mixed salad.

Tandoori Mushrooms.

Ingredients (for 6 servings)

16 medium-large white closed mushrooms
1 small tub yogurt
1 heaped tablespoon Garam Marsala powder
Pepper

Method

* Mix yogurt and Garam Marsala powder together in a small bowl.
* Cover the mushrooms with the yogurt mixture and leave in fridge for 2 hours.
* Heat grill to maximum.
* Spread the mushrooms in a tin and put under the very hot grill and cook until the yogurt covering is beginning to burn at the edges. Turn them over and cook the other side.
* Serve with mango chutney and an oriental salad.

Zsa Zsa's Red Cabbage

Ingredients (for 4-6 helpings)

1 medium sized red cabbage,
  cut into quarters and thinly sliced
1 large onion, sliced
1 large apple, cored and sliced but NOT peeled
2-3 tbsp of sugar

10 cl of red wine vinegar
50 g of dripping or rendered lamb or beef fat
25 cl of beef stock (water and a stock cube are okay)
Salt and pepper to taste
1 small carton of cream (optional)

Method

* Melt the fat in a large saucepan and, over a medium heat, fry the onion until edges are beginning to brown.
* Add the chopped red cabbage and stir around, ensuring all the pieces have a coating of fat. Cover the pan and cook on a low heat for 5 minutes.
* Now add the chopped apple and vinegar, stir in, cover the pan and leave on low heat for 10 minutes.
* Pour in the beef stock (stock cubes work very well, but if you use a cube, don't add salt!), bring to the boil, cover, turn down the heat to very low and simmer for about 1 hour. (If you like "casseroley" flavours, you may put the pot into a medium oven at this stage.) Check liquid from time to time, not letting the cabbage cook dry.
* As a final optional touch, add a small carton of cream, swirl in and put in a serving dish. Place this in a warm oven for around 15 minutes.

Zsa Zsa's red cabbage is delicious with grilled pork chops. Green beans and roast potatoes to accompany.

Puddings

Puddings

Vanilla Ice Cream

Good vanilla ice cream is made from:

100 g of caster sugar
4 egg yolks
30 cl of milk
30 cl of double cream
1 tsp of vanilla essence. .

Method

*   Beat the sugar and egg yolks together in a large bowl.
*   Heat the milk until almost boiling and pour little by little into the sugar/egg mixture, beating all the time.
*   Turn the sugar/egg/milk mixture into a saucepan and heat gently, together. Leave to cool.
*   Add the cream and mix well.
*   Turn mixture into one or more freezer bowls, cover and place in the freezer compartment of your fridge. Check after 10 minutes or so, and stir the freezing bits from the side into the middle. Repeat again every five minutes or so, until the mixture has set.

Of course, if you have an ice-cream maker, you just tip in the mixture and turn on.

Strawberry Ice Cream

Ingredients

500 g of strawberries
30 cl double cream
100 g caster sugar
Juice of one lemon

Method

*   In your food processor, purée the strawberries.
*   Put in the cream and sugar and briefly whiz.
*   Remove and put into a bowl
*   Cover and put in your freezer
*   Stir every 10 minutes, until mixture is set.

If you have an ice-cream maker, you simply put the puréed strawberries, sugar and cream into it and freeze/churn for about 20 minutes.

A quick alternative to ice-cream: half a kilo of strawberries, cut in half, a coffee cup of cherry or strawberry liqueur and a tub of yogurt. Put the halved strawberries in a bowl, add the liqueur and the yogurt, mix and chill for an hour.

South Carolina Ice Cream Dessert

Here's a lovely recipe from South Carolina, adapted for Cyprus ingredients.

Take about 75 g of unsalted butter, melt in a pan and sautée the following:

2 tsp sugar
Juice of 1 orange and 1 lemon
1 tbsp of grated orange rind
1 tbsp of lemon rind
1 tbsp of chopped Pecan Nuts or Walnuts.

Method

*   When the mixture is bubbling add 3 tbsp of Filfar or Orali orange liqueur, stir in and take off the heat.
*   In small fruit bowls put a scoop of vanilla ice cream, top with half a peeled peach and spoon over 2 tbsp of the orange sauce.

Quick. Easy. Delicious. Serves 6.

Chocolate Ice Cream

Ingredients

50 g of caster sugar
2 egg yolks
20 cl milk
15 cl double cream
150 g of dark, plain chocolate

Method

*   Beat the sugar and egg yolks together in a large bowl.
*   Heat the milk until almost boiling and pour little by little into the sugar/egg mixture, beating all the time.
*   Melt the chocolate in a bowl placed over a saucepan of boiling water.
*   Turn the sugar/egg/milk mixture into a saucepan and heat gently. Add the chocolate and mix carefully together. Leave to cool.
*   Add the cream and mix well.
*   Turn mixture into one or more freezer bowls, cover and place in the freezer compartment of your fridge. Check after 10 minutes or so, and stir the freezing bits from the side into the middle. Repeat again every five minutes or so, until the mixture has set.

The more bitter the chocolate the better this ice cream is.

Amoretti Chocolate Cream

Ingredients (serves 4-6)

200 g Mascapone or cream cheese
55 g fromage frais or yogurt
2 tbsp milk
4 tbsp caster sugar
4 tbsp Cyprus brandy
140 g good quality dark chocolate, melted in a bowl over simmering hot water
170 g Amoretti biscuits

Method

* Mix the cheese, fromage frais or yogurt and the milk in a bowl
* Add sugar and whisk until smooth
* Whisk in the brandy
* Whisk in the melted chocolate
* After reserving a few Amoretti for garnish, in a glass dish, put layers of biscuits and chocolate mixture.
* Chill for a minimum of one hour

Pamela's Lemon Yogurt Ice Cream

Ingredients

454 g carton of thick yogurt
150 g of double cream
100 g of caster sugar
Juice of two lemons

Method

*   Whisk together the yogurt, cream and sugar.
*   Add lemon juice and whisk more to ensure sugar is dissolved.
*   Freeze uncovered until mushy. Turn sides to centre and mix until smooth. Freeze until firm.

Pastry

My wife makes the best short crust pastry I know. She was taught how to do it by her Sussex country grandmother, and one of the secrets is never measuring anything out. So grandma's short-crust recipe, written down as faithfully as possible, is in my wife's recipe, which is my favourite.

Aunt Mary's Home-made Almond Tart

Ingredients (6-8 servings)

Short-crust pastry (120 g plain flour, 60 g butter, a few drops of water)
60 g **caster** sugar
60 g unsalted butter
1 large egg

30 g plain flour and half level tsp baking powder
60 g fresh ground almonds
Up to 1 tbsp milk
2-3 tbsp Cyprus Apricot or Mosphilla jam
Half cup icing sugar and a little water for glaze

Pastry: Method

* Sift the flour and into a bowl.
* Cut the butter into small chunks and lightly but quickly rub into the flour until the mixture is like breadcrumbs.
* Add a few drops of water and mix into flour/butter mixture until a good stiff dough is formed.
* Roll out to fit a 20cm round pastry tin, which you have rubbed with a little butter.
* Cut away surplus pastry and set aside.

Continued on next page.

Filling Method

* In a food processor, whip the butter and sugar until white and creamy.
* In a small bowl, beat the egg and add to the butter/sugar mixture, blending as you go.
* Slowly add flour and ground almonds, blending as you go.
* If mixture seems a little stiff, add a little milk to make a nice soft consistency.
* Now line the pastry case with the jam and then spread the filling over it, smoothing it out evenly.
* Roll out the remaining pastry, cut into thin strips and make a lattice pattern on the top of the tart.
* Bake in the middle of the oven heated to 180°C for around 30 minutes, when mixture should have risen and become quite firm.
* While the tart is baking, mix the half cup of icing sugar with a little water until a smooth paste is formed, thin enough to brush over the tart.
* Remove tart from oven, brush over the icing sugar glaze and return to the oven for around five minutes. Serve hot or cold—it's equally delicious.

Le Tarte Tatin

Ingredients for 6 servings
Pastry
250 g plain flour
1 tbsp sugar
115 g unsalted butter
12.5 cl lukewarm water, slightly salted

Apple Mixture:
6 firm dessert apples, peeled, cored and quartered
250 g sugar
3 tbsp melted unsalted butter
Several pinches cinnamon powder

Method

* Knead the flour, butter and sugar lightly and quickly.
* Gently pour in the salted water a little at a time and continue kneading.
* Press the mixed dough into a ball and put in the refrigerator for an hour or so.
* Now chop apple quarters into two or three pieces.
* In a non-stick skillet or two handled oven proof frying pan heat half the sugar until it caramelises, making sure it doesn't burn.
* Arrange the chopped apples over the caramel, sprinkle the sugar and the powdered cinnamon over and then evenly pour over the melted butter.
* Return the pan to the stove, cover and cook on a medium heat for around five minutes.
* While you are doing this roll out the pastry into a circle large enough to cover the pan.
* Remove pan from stove and fit pastry over the apples, tucking the pastry edge down the side of the pan.
* Put pan into a pre-heated medium oven and bake for 30 minutes, until pastry is brown.
* Remove from oven and immediately (and quickly) invert on to a serving dish.
* If the top is not well caramelised, put dish under a hot grill for a few minutes.
* Serve warm with whipped cream.

Bread & Butter Pudding

Ingredients for 4 portions

2 2-day old long (20 cm/8") soft bread rolls, cut in half lengthways or 6 slices of old white bread crusts removed.
3 eggs
3 level tbsp caster sugar
25 cl cream
25 cl milk
100 g butter
Grated lemon peel
1 cup sultanas

Method

*   Butter the rolls or bread quite generously.
*   Place the rolls/bread in a buttered baking dish.
*   Sprinkle the grated lemon peel and the sultanas over.
*   Beat the eggs with a little milk and half the sugar.
*   Whisk the cream into the egg/milk mixture adding remaining milk.
*   Pour over the rolls/bread, sprinkle remaining sugar over the top and bake in a medium oven (180°C) for about half an hour.

Serve with cream or vanilla ice-cream and a glass of dessert wine.

Peaches in Wine

*   Peel and slice into segments one large peach for each person.
*   Place in a bowl and sprinkle with plenty of caster sugar.
*   Cover with a good fruity white or red wine, cover and put in the fridge for an hour or two.
*   Serve in dishes or glasses, making sure everyone gets his or her share of the juice!
*   A dollop of whipped cream and a Lady's Finger or two may be added if you're feeling really wicked.

Cherries

Unless you are simply serving up a bowl of washed fresh cherries, it's best to remove the stones. You can use an olive or cherry stoner if you like, but I find it easiest to split the cherry between thumb and forefinger and squeeze the stone out. TIP: do this in the sink, because cherry juice both squirts and stains.

Steep the pitted cherries in Cyprus cherry liqueur (about a coffeecupful) for an hour or two and serve with whipped cream.

Or drain and use in a recipe like the one on the next page.

Per's Pudding

Ingredients (for 6-8 portions)

2 medium-large eggs
200 grams of caster sugar
125 grams of plain or village flour
Half teaspoon of baking powder
250 grams of pitted cherries, steeped as above, drained
About 100 grams of very cold unsalted butter

Method

* Heat the oven to 175°C.
* Rub a little butter over a 28-30cms round pastry tin, non-stick for preference. Dust with a sprinkling of flour.
* In a food processor, blend the eggs and sugar until very creamy and whitish. Or beat with a whisk.
* Add the flour and baking powder and whiz until blended.
* Spoon the mixture into the pastry tin and spread evenly.
* Dot the drained cherries all over the mixture.
* Take butter from the fridge and flake off very thin slivers to cover the top of the mixture.
* Bake for around 30-35 minutes, until top is golden brown and crisp and the mixture is cooked.
* Serve warm or cold, with cream, ice-cream or a fruit coulis - fresh apricot, for example (10-12 stoned and peeled apricots, whizzed for a few seconds in a blender with a little sugar and a coffee cup of Cyprus apricot liqueur).

This delicious variation on a sponge cake theme can use a variety of fruits - strawberries, chopped apple (with skins), apricots, peaches, even raisins. Good the following day, too, if there's any left!

Chocolate Cake

Ingredients for the cake

170 g of self-raising flour or plain flour mixed with a half tsp of Baking Powder
1 heaped tbsp of cocoa powder
3 tbsp boiling water
170 g unsalted butter
170 g **caster** sugar
3 eggs
Half tsp vanilla essence

Method

* Heat oven to 180°C.
* Grease and line with greaseproof paper two 20 cm (8") diameter shallow sponge tins.
* Put the cocoa powder into a small bowl and thoroughly mix in the boiling water.
* In your food processor blend the butter and sugar until it is a creamy ball.
* Tip in the cocoa mixture and whizz until blended.
* Add the eggs, one by one, and the vanilla essence, whizzing all the time.
* Add the flour, little by little, whizzing until you have a nice smooth mixture
* Remove and spoon into the two sponge tins.
* Bake in centre of oven for about 25 minutes.
* When done, let cool for a few minutes and remove from tins.
* Prepare the chocolate cream.

Continued on next page.

Chocolate Cake - Continued.

Ingredients for the chocolate cream

30 g cocoa powder
100 g icing sugar
50 g unsalted butter
3 des-sp water
60 g **caster** sugar

Method

* Mix the cocoa and icing sugar thoroughly in a mixing bowl.
* Put the butter, water and **caster** sugar in a small saucepan.
* Heat, stirring all the time, until the butter and sugar have dissolved completely. Remove and put into the bowl containing the cocoa and icing sugar.
* Mix well and allow to cool.
* Use the chocolate cream to spread between the two sponges and on the top and around the sides.

For "poor man's Black Forest Gateau", before spreading the chocolate cream put a layer of black cherry or raspberry jam on one of the sponges, spread the chocolate cream on top of that and then spread a layer of thick whipped cream. Spread the remaining chocolate cream on the top of the second sponge and place it carefully on the top.

Cyprus Orange & Almond Flan

Ingredients

Rind and juice of 3 large or 4 medium oranges
4 eggs
125 g freshly ground almonds
175 g **caster** sugar
1 tbsp Cyprus brandy or orange liqueur

Method

* Take a large, round, shallow pastry tin (arounds 30 cms diameter), and rub some butter over the inside. Sprinkle flour on and shake until it is settled all over.
* Wash and dry the oranges. With a fine grater, carefully grate the rind and set aside. Halve and squeeze them. Set the juice aside.
* Separate the eggs and beat the yolks with 125 g of the sugar and the rind until creamy and yellowy.
* Beat in the ground almonds slowly.
* Beat the egg whites until stiff and fold gently into the mixture. Spoon out into the baking dish and put in the centre of the oven, heated to 220°C.
* After 15 minutes turn down oven to 170°C and cook for about 15 minutes more. Remove from the oven and cool for 10 minutes, then remove from the tin.
* Mix the remaining sugar with orange juice and liqueur or brandy and sprinkle over the flan.

Kati Meri

Ingredients

300 g of flour
1 tsp baking powder
3 eggs
4 tbsp Cyprus brandy

2 tbsp **caster** sugar
25 cl of "honey syrup" (see **Method**)
60 g of chopped almonds
1 tsp of cinnamon

Method

* In a large bowl, mix flour and baking powder. Make a well in the centre.
* Beat eggs, sugar and brandy and slowly dribble in to the flour, kneading well to make a pastry dough. Put in fridge for 30 minutes and then knead again.
* On a floured board, roll out the pastry into a thin sheet.
* Cut into strips, squares or whatever shapes you want.
* In a large deep frying pan or saucepan heat a litre of oil until very hot.
* Drop the pastry shapes into the hot oil and cook until they are golden. Remove and dry on kitchen paper. Place on a warmed dish.
* Now take a cupful of Cyprus honey, put in a small pan and stir in a half cup of hot water. Heat and simmer until you have a nice syrup.
* Pour syrup over the pastries, sprinkle over the chopped almonds and pinches of cinnamon.

Serve with Cyprus coffee.

Kaiserschmarr'n   (4-6 good helpings)

Put into a small cup:
> 2 tbsp raisins
> 4 tbsp rum
> Soak the raisins in the rum for ▯ hour

Add:
> 50 cl milk
> ⅛ tsp vanilla extract
> Then gradually add: 150 g flour, sifted
> Add the pre-soaked raisins and rum to the batter.
> Carefully fold in: 5 stiffly beaten egg whites

Beat until creamy:
> 4 egg yolks (separated from the whites)
> 50 g sugar
> **Several pinches of salt**

Method

* Melt 1 tbsp of butter in a large non-stick fry pan.
* Pour into the pan half the above batter (the batter should be no more than 1 cm thick) and cook for 4 minutes over a low heat until the bottom side is light brown.
* Slide the pancake onto a plate and put a second tablespoon of butter in the pan. Bake the other side of the pancake in the butter.
* Repeat the procedure for the second half of the batter.
* Then, with a fork, tear the two pancakes apart into 6-8 pieces (or 5 cm squares).
* Put more butter in the pan if needed and return the pieces from both pancakes to the pan.
* Turn the pieces a few times to ensure that the batter is cooked through.
* Dust with powdered sugar and serve hot (in the pan) with stewed fruit such as plums, apples, peaches or fruit mixture on the side.

Crullers

Something Swedish, to hand around with the coffee ...

Ingredients to make around 30

4 egg yolks
50 g caster sugar
Quarter tsp salt
1 tbsp Cyprus brandy
Grated rind of one lemon
2 tbsp butter
100 g flour

Method

* In a blender, whiz the egg yolks, sugar, salt, brandy and lemon rind. Mix in butter and flour and whiz until you have a good ball of dough.
* Remove, wrap in cling-film and refrigerate for an hour or two.
* Roll out the dough to about 3mm thickness. Cut into diagonal strips 3cm x 10cm.
* Make a slit in the middle and pull one end through it.
* In a deep heavy pan, heat half a litre or so of vegetable oil. Deep fry a few Krullers at a time until they are golden.
* Remove, pat the oil off with kitchen paper and dip in caster sugar.

Meringues

When asked: "You gave a recipe for mayonnaise, using egg yolks, but what do you suggest I do with the egg whites?", I reply as follows. "Generally I use 3-4 eggs for the mayonnaise and keep the whites (they'll stay quite all right for some days in the fridge) to make meringues, which dinner party guests and visitors seem to adore".

Method

* For every 2 egg whites, you need 115 g of **caster** sugar.
* Whisk the egg whites until pretty stiff. Add half the sugar and carry on whisking until the texture is smooth and forms peaks when the whisk is taken out.
* Add the remaining sugar carefully and mix in with a spoon.
* Line a flat baking tray with grease-proof paper, non-stick if you can get it, and spoon the meringue mix into small mounds on the paper. Make them round with a spoon.
* Sprinkle with **caster** sugar and bake in a *very, very slow* oven (around 75°C) for 3-4 hours.

Serving suggestions

Whip one small carton of cream until stiff and put a dessertspoonful between two cooled meringues. Serve with puréed peaches or apricots, or a hot chocolate sauce.

Wine and Food

"A meal without wine is like a day without sunshine"

The French-born gastronome, Anthelme Brillat-Savarin (1775 – 1826), wrote the above line and all I can say to it is "Amen".   I do draw the line at wine for breakfast, however, though just now and then at some event, celebration or other, where there has been a splendiferous spread of the Great British Breakfast, including Kedgeree, Devilled Kidneys and a slice of steak or two, I have quaffed the odd glass of Ale.

If you have read, scanned or skimmed through these pages, you will notice frequent use of wine, spirits and liqueurs in the recipes. In other words, I think that alcoholic beverages are virtually indispensable accesories to good cooking. And what fun we who live in Cyprus can have, with every kind of vinous and spiritous concoction available to us at remarkably modest prices! If you are visiting these shores and want to take a bottle or two back with you, for both degustatory and culinary use, then I suggest: a bottle each of Cyprus Brandy, Fino Cyprus sherry, Orange Liqueur and several of the good red wines you have isolated and enjoyed during your stay here.

As for drinking wine with food – well! To me they are *essential companions.*

As to which wine – this is entirely up to you!   There is no mystique about it. Drink the wine you like with the food you like.   And if they don't always match, what a wonderful time you can have finding food and wine that does.

Index

Acknowledgements

For the fact that it's here, in your hands, I have to thank :-

Kyriacos Jacovides, managing director of the Cyprus Mail for publishing it.

The patient **Sue Kyriacou** for being a tower of strength in typing, re-typing, editing and checking recipes

Alex Pays for the computer type-setting and page layout, as well as much re-positioning of words and pictures.

Alyana Cazalet for doing the cover and super illustrations, which are much better, in my view, than a lot of fancy photographs which are often phoney and which you can never hope to reproduce in real life.

Glen Ayres for the drawings of my kitchen and the herbs on pages 16, 17, 19 and 20. There are five drawings/engravings from old books in my collection on pages 7, 18, 38, 87 and 125

Ann Ryan and **Mary Skinner** for checking, re-checking and proof reading.

For the fact that I can cook at all I have to thank so many people. Unfortunately some of them, like my mother, are no longer in this particular world, as, probably, are the school chefs and some of those on various RAF stations, who taught me what murdered food tasted and looked like. Whether they are all in the same place I am not sure.

My first wife, Tina, introduced me to Middle Eastern cookery, for which I am eternally grateful. My second, Mary, a discerning "customer" and excellent cook, has shared so many meals, in many places and has put up with more than 25 years of my cooking, as have our children. All have been (generally) appreciative of my efforts, and have given me constant encouragement.

I am grateful to countless hotel chefs and restaurant and taverna keepers, for putting something in front of me that I wanted to know more about and for being willing to tell me. Then there are far greater cooks/writers than I, who have inspired me, through wonderful books and superb recipes. In the field of Middle Eastern cooking, in my opinion, Claudia Roden has no peers. For his friendly, bucolic approach to food, wine and cookery, I adore Keith Floyd. For perfectly correct and utterly perfect recipes of France and the Mediterranean region, Elizabeth David is another great inspiration.

But perhaps the greatest encouragement of all is that every week I have to write at least two food columns, which causes me to spend many hours researching, reading, experimenting, trying out and writing. Despite commitments of seven days a week I am basically lazy and without these deadlines the recipes wouldn't exist, so thanks to anybody who has ever asked me to write an article for them.

And finally, a thank you to you, dear reader, who have paid good money to read this humble effort. Part of your payment for the book will be donated to a cause very, very close to me (like outside my back door): a Sanctuary I help my wife run under the Charitable Association name, "Friends of the Cyprus Donkey".

Patrick Skinner
4772 Vouni Village
Limassol District
Cyprus   September 1998